Putting Movement Into Your Life

a beyond fitness primer

Maxine Sheets-Johnstone

In her first life, Maxine Sheets-Johnstone was a dancer/choreographer, professor of dance/dance scholar. In her second and ongoing life, she is a philosopher who taught periodically in the Philosophy Department at the University of Oregon in the 1990s and who holds a continuing Courtesy Professor appointment in the department. She has written over 70 articles in arts, humanities, and science journals, and has published eight other books, including *The Roots of Thinking*, *The Primacy of Movement*, and *The Corporeal Turn: An Interdisciplinary Reader*. She was awarded a Distinguished Fellowship at the Institute of Advanced Study at Durham University, UK, in 2007, an Alumni Achievement Award by the School of Education, University of Wisconsin in 2011, and was honored with a Scholar's Session by the Society for Phenomenology and Existential Philosophy in 2012.

ISBN-13: 978-1497476950
ISBN-10: 149747695X

Table Of Contents

An Invitation

This book invites you on a journey. Ordinarily, you have your mind on your destination when you start a journey. You commonly experience all the moving about in preparation and then the actual movement of travel itself as a means to an end, namely, getting where you want to be—whether you're driving or flying or bussing or biking. When you read a book that captures your attention, you go on a similar kind of journey in terms of actual movement. You're engrossed in a narrative that keeps you flipping pages, one after the next, until the very end. All that page-turning movement through the book is simply a means to an end—your desired arrival on the next page, and then the next, and then the next . . .

This book invites you to go on a different kind of journey, one in which the center point of interest and attention is not a destination or a narrative. The words you read describe a journey through all the myriad possibilities of putting actual real-time movement into your real-time life. In other words, the words themselves are the means to an end, which is the reality of movement itself.

The first chapter introduces you to moving, something you've obviously done all your life and continue to do but commonly don't notice, or not for long anyway. If you accept the invitation, you'll be launched on a nonlinear journey, for along the way—and even in the beginning chapter—you'll have the option of making little side trips, optional detours that involve a different kind of page-turning. When you open these pages, you'll be led to new ways of thinking about movement. What's written in these pages is intended to make you pause and ponder, just as you might pause and ponder over a vista or smell or piece of music in order to deepen your experience of it. The little side journeys are indeed intended as reflective stopping posts offering slow food for thought about movement. They are called Ponderabilia, the suffix *abilia* coming from the Latin practice of forming an adjective from a verb. May you find slow food for thought about movement, something fit to be pondered and worth pondering, hence ponderable!

Now in light of movement being the center of attention, a major question is whether you read the book in one sitting or spread the sittings out over several days and even several weeks, actually stopping to explore precisely what is being described. If you take each successive invitation to move seriously, you'll bring a wealth of possibilities into your life. Just as when you take time to savor something or to learn something new, so you'll be taking time to explore possibilities that literally move you to move. Moreover as noted above, the point is not the reading but the moving that the reading is describing. What you're invited to explore by way of the descriptions is not some kind of esoteric movement practice but everyday movement which, as you might by now guess, turns out to be potentially more interesting, pleasurable, and downright fun than you ever before imagined. So just as you wouldn't want to have breakfast, lunch, and dinner all in one sitting, you would not want to put movement into your life in one fell swoop but step by step as it were, enjoying each step forward on its own. In short, you're invited to spread the read out rather than gorge yourself in one sitting.

Finally, you might make notes and comments of your own as you side-trip your way through the Ponderabilia, journeying on as you choose along whatever thought-filled lines of movement suit your fancy.

Chapter 1

FEELING YOUR ALIVENESS: AN EXPERIENCE NOT TO BE MISSED

Putting Movement Into Your Life is both about and not about getting into shape. It has nothing to do with a scheduled program of exercises, but everything to do with moving—and not limiting movement to particular times during the week.

Playing paddle ball, jogging, taking an aerobics or yoga class—these are all vitalizing activities. But what happens during the rest of the day and week? Let's say you're up sixteen hours a day, seven days a week, and that you exercise a total of seven to ten hours a week. What's going on in the way of 'shape' during the remaining 102 to 105 hours? Sure, you feel great during and after jogging or swimming. Are there ways of renewing these feelings of vitality throughout the day—short of jogging or swimming all over again? Can you recapture the sense of aliveness you felt when you were playing paddle ball or tennis? More than this, are there ways of drawing back a moment from doing the laundry, studying a report, weeding the garden, or even talking, and coming back to the task refreshed and vibrant?

Putting Movement Into Your Life is saying, "Yes, there are!" It is saying that moving doesn't have to be reserved to special times and places; an enhanced sense of vitality doesn't have to be confined to jogging paths and gymnasiums. Being alive is something you are all the time. Why not enjoy it more often by feeling it more often? Feeling alive is not some quirky kind of self-indulgence unless cultivated to the point of doing nothing else. Putting Movement Into Your Life is not about doing nothing else.

If you've ever had to freeze on the spot or play dead, you know it's hard to keep perfectly still. It's hard to keep your eyelids from fluttering and your chest from going up and down with each breath. And unless you're stretched out horizontally, it's hard too to keep from swaying this way and that. Of course you're not usually aware of such movements. Blinking, breathing, and swaying aren't something you make happen— they happen to you, and for the most part go unnoticed. But if you were hooked on moving and on noticing movement . . .

Moving is at the heart of being alive. Rocks don't go forth in search of a mate and water doesn't flow forth in search of something to eat. Eating, sheltering, defending, mating, playing, and exploring are animate experiences; all creatures make their living by moving about. While aspects of our human movement repertoire are shared with other mammals, our overall capacities and patterns of movement are peculiar to us. Like all creatures, we have a particular kinetic domain or repertoire of movement possibilities.

In the nonhuman animal world there are few constraints upon movement. In a general sense, nonhuman animals do what they feel like doing when they feel like doing it. In contrast, the wherever, whatever, and however of human movement are restricted in one way and another by unwritten rules of culture. What you move in an office or church is different from what you move on a dance floor or playing field. Not only that but only certain ways of moving those certain parts are considered proper. Skipping, for example, is not one of several acceptable ways of crossing the street—at least for adults. Neither is rehearsing a tennis serve or drawing imaginary circles with your fingertips an alternative way of passing the time while waiting in line at the supermarket or for a bus. What you move, and how and where you move it, are limited by cultural rules your adult body knows by heart.

Take range of movement, for example. No matter how acceptable a given movement, there are limits to how much of it is allowed. Standing with your weight on one leg, for instance, is quite acceptable. Tapping the ground with your free foot is fine too. But raising the whole of your foot off the ground between taps—to say nothing of intermittently entwining it around your standing leg—is likely to get you a few stares. Legs and feet—male and female ones—are generally expected to remain symmetrically close for life, to stand or fall together as it were. Creating out-of-the-ordinary bodily shapes is typically looked upon as weird. You can raise your arm overhead and move it about to wave to someone or to hail a taxi, but short of a someone or a taxi at the end of the movement—well, other people's eyebrows are likely to go up along with your arm.

Yet suppose you did feel urges from time to time to raise your arms overhead and move them about. Suppose you felt like stretching them overhead in the middle of a theater lobby during intermission or while you were waiting your turn at the bank. If you ever gave in to such urges, you'd likely be considered an exhibitionist or a looney.

Normal people accommodate such urges in a culturally appropriate place, a place where that kind of movement is allowed: a park, dance studio, their own home, or a gymnasium. Only in Hollywood films and Broadway musicals can you break out into movement wherever you are—and seemingly, into whatever and however much movement you want.

Why should movement be so curtailed? What, after all, is the matter with moving your arms overhead in public places—or skipping across the street, for that matter? The answer most probably is that movement should not call attention to itself, or more positively, that movement should call attention to itself only in places where it's supposed to: a football field, a basketball court, or a theater stage; in other words, only in places where spectators are a bona fide part of the kinetic proceedings. People in a theater lobby or bank aren't supposed to be spectators of movement. To turn them into spectators is to intrude on everyday neutral public spaces and make them into showplaces. In doing that, you literally make a spectacle of yourself and embarrass other people in the process.

But consider the following true story.

When teaching senior citizens some years ago, I often encouraged them to enlarge on their everyday movements, particularly swinging their arms more fully as they walked down the street. Ordinarily adults keep their arms close to their bodies as they walk. They don't really indulge in movement. The response to the fuller arm swings over and over again was "What an experience!" The senior citizens loved it. All they needed to get them going was an awareness of the possibility and the sanction that it was okay to move like that.

Do senior citizens feel less at stake? Are they less jaded than the young or middle-aged? Do they care less what other people think? The answer is possibly 'yes' to all three questions, but the answers are really less important than the significance of the fuller movement itself: it feels good to move and to move in that way. It feels good simply to be alive. Movement can give you an instant sense of aliveness. *(Ponderabilia 1: On Movement and Feeling Alive)*

Now it's not as if you weren't alive or didn't realize you're alive until you started doing some life-proclaiming movement. It's only that this capacity of movement to awaken a sense of aliveness is usually dormant. Movement in everyday life is a means to an end, not an end in itself. Never mind that writing a letter, getting to a meeting, washing dishes, even conversing with others, literally hang on movement; none of them is done for the sake of moving. In consequence, none calls attention to aliveness.

This fact of everyday life brings us back to the senior citizen story. Swinging your arms while walking is not a bizarre accompaniment to striding legs on their way to the store. On the contrary, swinging arms and striding legs are a natural coordination of the body, an integral part of walking: if left to their own devices, your arms normally swing back and forth when you walk, balancing in contralateral fashion the movement of your legs. Stretching arms overhead is also a natural human movement. Swinging the arms and stretching them overhead are part of our movement repertoire; they are built-ins of our being human.

11

Feeling your aliveness is not then a matter of learning a new set of movements but of rediscovering your own. You reclaim something that's been there all along but which you've been too busy to notice.

It's not just arm and leg movements that need rediscovery. It's movement of the whole body. Pelvic movements—in fact movements of the entire torso—are generally expected to keep a low public profile. One false move here and you're classified as a degenerate: circular, side to side, or tilting movements are typically viewed as seductive, lewd, sexy, immoral, and the like.

But have you ever thought of how many times you make circles with different parts of your body in the course of a day? Or have you ever thought of the difference between making circles with your arm and hand, as when you're stirring a batter or wiping a dish—or with your heels, as when you're jogging (imagine a piece of chalk being attached to your heels as you jog and you'll discover circular motion)—and making circles with your hips? If you drew arm-stirring batter circles and hip circles at the same time, getting hips and arm to move concurrently, you'd find typical classifications and judgments suddenly defused. Drawing circles with the hips would become simply an interesting movement possibility and engaging pattern of movement, a particular flow of bodily energy that has a certain direction, tempo, and range—not unlike the direction, tempo, and range of your batter-stirring arm.

What any movement might mean depends in part on how you do it, but in part too on how you choose to perceive it. In either case, what Marianne Moore said of a poem can also be said of any movement: it can simply be. It doesn't have to mean anything at all in the sense of referring to some particular state of affairs or state of being. You can make circles with your hips—or with your eyes or with your knees—without it meaning that you're licentious or lustful or weird in some way, or that you're anti-cultural or in general a miscreant when it comes to movement.

Waking up to the joys of moving doesn't mean going against the grain. It means waking up to being alive. Part of that awareness is rooted in the discovery that sensing and moving go together. In our busy world of everyday activities, the movement side of that duo is swallowed up in the task at hand: you watch the nail disappearing into the wood rather than feel the dynamics of the hammering movements themselves. When a skill is being learned—handling a tennis racquet, coordinating the use of pedals in playing the piano—or relearned as in walking again after a stroke, the situation is different. Here you become finely attentive to movement. You notice the direction and intensity of your arm swing in a forehand drive, or the weight, balance, and sustained effort necessary to putting one foot in front of the other in walking. In such situations what you sense is movement itself.

It's obvious then that if you're going to put movement into your life, what's essential first of all is noticing movement in the midst of its very happening. As with wine tasting, you have to become aware of the sensory experience itself. In this kind of experience, movement is no longer getting you to a meeting, into a car, or into a standing position. It's not getting you anywhere except in touch with yourself. Like any other sensory experience, this one has a name. It's called kinesthesia—from the Greek kinein (to move) and aisthesis (perception). *(Ponderabilia 2: It's Amazing!)* It's actually this sensory awareness that keeps you on course in everyday life. You don't have to gauge your movement every step of the way in walking any more than you have to monitor every stroke of your toothbrush when brushing your teeth. Originally, of course, you did have to pay attention, you did have to notice what you were doing, but all of these capacities have long since become part of your movement repertoire—your compendium of "I cans." The point is that if you're going to cultivate feelings of aliveness, you have to get back to noticing yourself in movement. You have to become re-acquainted with your kinesthetic self.

Exercise programs at times face you in the opposite direction. Rather than encouraging kinesthetic awareness, they encourage you to take your mind off yourself, to turn your attention away from what is considered to be drudging, boring labor. You're encouraged to make up fantasies while you're moving, for example, or to concentrate on what a good thing you're doing for your body, or to lose yourself in portable music. Waking up to the joys of moving means going with the movement. It means kinesthetically feeling rather than fantasizing, thinking, or being elsewhere than in the movement itself. It means kinesthetically feeling the movement flow forth in the particular qualitative way it is flowing forth. It means you are alive in the here and now, feeling the qualitative dynamic realities of your moving body, the quickness, the expansiveness, the intensity, and so on. In the process, you may notice differences: too much effort, for instance, when you're bending over this time around or the free movement ride you get in generating momentum—as when you swing your leg from the hip instead of the knee. When you listen to the movement, you stay with the movement, and you end by noticing yourself. This noticing of yourself is not a matter of wallowing in bodily experiences but of discriminating qualitatively among them.

Noticing is only half the story, the sensing half. To put movement into your life, you can start either by noticing movement or by moving. In other words, you can make differences as well as notice them. At whichever end you start, you end up discovering how sensing and moving go together—always.

Making differences livens things up. Making differences means unplanting yourself—figuratively as well as literally. The more sedentary you are the more plant-like you become. But the more habitual you become, the more plant-like you become also. Your movement repertoire reduces to a set of tropisms, patterned responses repeated over and over and over again.

People often remark on the many books they haven't read or the number of countries they haven't visited or the sums of money they haven't made. Have you ever thought of all the movement you haven't experienced? We don't ordinarily think of making differences because we're task-oriented and movement-oblivious. But we can all do the same old things in a new and innovative way. Not only can we walk in different ways, we can make a bed, close a drawer, wait in line, and even ride in a car in different ways. In so doing, you can figuratively as well as literally give a new twist to your life.

Making differences and noticing differences. This book is about both. It's about surprising yourself in the course of everyday habits and making a habit of surprising yourself.

Chapter 2

OPENING UP TO MOVEMENT: YOUR MOVEMENT PULSE AND HOW TO TAKE IT

The way in which you do something reveals a certain style of movement, a style as individualized as your thumbprint. This is because movement is a process, a dynamic happening you create every time you move. Everyone from infancy to old age leaves movement prints about. They can't help it; it's in the way they do things—the way they lift, throw, clean, chase, smile, drive, and even fish.

A Few First Words About Movement

Movement tells us a story about ourselves in terms of our individual styles of moving—and thereby hangs the tale that is the ultimate subject of this chapter: your movement pulse. It's as accessible and easy to take as the one the doctor takes. But before we begin listening in on it, we need to say a few first words about movement as a dynamic process and the possibility of lighting up your awareness of it.

Dynamic happenings may be relatively small, brief, and seemingly one-dimensional as in threading a needle or flicking the TV dial to another channel; or they may be as large, lengthy, and multidimensional as getting into a car and settling into the driver's seat.

The possible dynamics of any one of these everyday happenings are virtually limitless. It's why movement is so fascinating and a source of endless appeal.

To become aware of what you're doing is actually not to become aware of what you're doing at all. It's to become aware of how you're doing the what; it's to notice the dynamics of the kinetic process in which you're involved. This is because nine times out of ten, you're already well aware of what you're doing—washing the car, beating the eggs, talking on the phone. You don't need to remind yourself, nor do you have to look into the matter more closely to find out what it is you're up to. In fact, very rarely do you ever surprise yourself—especially to the point where you'd say, "Ah! So that's what I'm doing!" to someone who comes along and announces, "You're sawing wood!" To become aware of what you're doing is thus actually to shift attention from the customary what to the less-than-customary how of your doings. With this subtle shift in attention—who is to know but you?—you begin noticing yourself in the process of moving. *(Ponderabilia 3: On Behavior and Movement)*

This noticing of yourself is not self-conscious in the usual sense. Usually when you're self-conscious, you're uncomfortable—sometimes even hamstrung. You're unable to continue doing what you're doing with any sense of fluency or confidence. This kind of self-consciousness is induced by Others Watching. In noticing yourself in movement, self-consciousness is a matter of your own attentiveness, not someone else's. You're simply feeling yourself in action; you're listening in on your own energy flow; you're experiencing the dynamic happening that is you-in-movement.

Now you can go with this happening and carefully eavesdrop on it, or you can play with it. In other words, you can attend fully to the feel of the movement as it flows forth, or you can, in the best tradition, tinker with it. When you utilize your skills in the manner of a master listener and tinkerer, you're taking your movement pulse—and more.

What does it mean to listen to movement?

When you want someone to pay attention to something visual, you say, "Look!" When you want someone to hear something special, you say, "Listen!" Unfortunately, there's not an analogous everyday word for noticing movement—from the inside, that is. Noticing movement from the outside is a visual noticing (which is all to the good too, but not the subject here). What's needed is an everyday word that calls attention to the experience of movement as a kinesthetically-felt happening.

What would you think if someone said "Feel!" to you in the same way they said "Look!" or "Listen!"?

Feeling has so many meanings. When you touch something, you feel it; when something hurts, you feel it; when you love someone, you feel it; when it's hot outside, you feel it; when someone shoves you, you feel it. All of these feelings are common everyday awarenesses: they are first-nature to us. Feelings of self-movement are also first-nature, or at least they can be when and if we heed them. Usually though, we feel them in the background. We seldom give them first-nature attention.

The first thing then is to differentiate between feeling vaguely and feeling prominently in a kinesthetic sense. There's a difference between implicit feelings of movement—as when you know you're brushing your teeth even as you're thinking of what you'll wear this morning or whether the car will start—and explicit feelings of movement—as when you feel the brushing movements themselves. Once the distinction has been made between in-the-foreground feelings of movement and in-the-background feelings of movement, a name can be given to first-nature attention.

The word 'listen', in addition to the general, all-senses word 'notice', is a good one. Listening has both the sense of paying attention and of heeding something in a focused way over a period of time. Moreover the something heeded in listening is not an object in the usual visual sense of objects. Melodic sounds or the whistling of the wind, for example, are not something you can pick up to examine but something you must catch on the wing in order to grasp.

Yet dynamic processes are not thereby flash-in-the-pan happenings; on the contrary, they take time to heed. They might thus require some getting used to. They don't give off the instant bang so commonly sought in our lives today. On the other hand, listening to yourself in movement is the most instant experience you could ever have. You don't have to do anything special to get it. It's not like going to Disneyland or Europe where you have to make arrangements beforehand. It's not even like having to put the CD in the slot before you can listen to the music or having to get dressed before you can go outside. You can listen to yourself without lifting a finger—in the same way you can listen to the wind without getting an earful. Kinesthetic happenings are going on all the time. But more of that later. For now, armed with a movement vocabulary, you're going to lift fingers and more. You're going to learn how to take your movement pulse.

Brushing Your Teeth

You brush your teeth every morning. It's a simple, repetitive process. The direction of the movement changes as you go along; your grip and the force of your grip change too. There's actually a little drama of dynamic happenings in brushing your teeth, which is why brushing your teeth is an ideal activity to use to take your movement pulse.

Chances are you never pay much attention anymore to these dynamic happenings. Tooth-brushing is second-nature—a thoroughly engrained habit. When you first learned though—when you first acquired the technique—you paid attention. You might even have struggled to get the brush going consistently and in the right direction if you were looking in a mirror at the same time and were trying to coordinate your movements with those of your mirror image. Once you mastered the technique, however, you didn't have to give it a second thought.

But even habits are open to variation . . .

For example, suppose you're late in getting up and you're rushing to get to work or to school on time. What happens when you brush your teeth? You brush faster—and perhaps less thoroughly. Chances are too you hold the toothbrush more tightly. In fact, chances are that the more you rush, the faster you brush and the harder you grip. Instead of a fluid, brisk motion, there's a choppy, tight motion.

20

Do you have to increase your tension to move faster?

Not necessarily. But in practice, almost always.

The point is that the more excess tension, the less likely that the movement is efficient. To be efficient, the channels of movement need to be open. Just as a river doesn't flow when its course is jammed, so movement doesn't flow when its channels are jammed. In taking your movement pulse, you'll find out whether your energy channels are open or jammed shut with tension.

How do you usually brush your teeth? You pick up your toothbrush and close in on it with your fingers. When you actually begin brushing, there's a tendency to grip it more firmly, so firmly at times that were someone to try to snatch your toothbrush from you, you'd be pulled bodily forward along with the brush. Since there's no such someone hanging about and since your brush is not self-ambulatory, there's actually no need to fear its taking off without you.

When you brush your teeth tomorrow morning (or this evening), notice how tightly you're holding onto your brush. Then make some differences:

Loosen your hold—just a bit, the merest fraction. Does this loosening alter your ability to proceed with the task at hand?

Let go a little bit more. Are you still brushing effectively?

And then a bit more. Still getting the job done?

Now see with how little effort you can hold onto the brush while continuing to brush your teeth—the absolute minimum necessary to holding the brush and completing the job.

By making differences and listening to the differences you've made, you've monitored the flow of your movement. If you've followed through on this simple experience of noticing and letting go, letting go and noticing, you'll have taken your movement pulse several times over. It will tell you something about yourself and about the relationship between tension and movement. If you listen carefully, you'll get an instamatic movement print; and you'll discover the style of moving that is you in the act of brushing your teeth. *(Ponderabilia 4: Pulsing With Life!)*

Most people find they can make a string of slight decreases in tension without losing their toothbrush. But suppose you found from the first that you were holding the brush with minimum tension; if you loosened your grip at all, you'd drop the brush. If this was your experience, your movement pulse isn't in need of tinkering at all, at least not in this instance. Just be sure you're not misleading yourself by too hasty trials and too immodest decreases. Be sure you really are making progressively small decreases in pressure, the smallest you can possibly detect.

It's likely that from one brushing to the next, there'll be remarkable differences in your movement pulse. Some mornings are less frenzied than others. Some mornings there may be no slight decreases to make; sometimes your movement pulse will be telling you a fluid, uncluttered story to begin with. If you listen carefully, you'll be able to distinguish more tense initial brushings from less tense ones.

Now, what happens when you do release pressure? What happens when you unweld yourself from your toothbrush?

A slow-motion wave of relief washes over you. Your breathing drops to deeper levels in the exhalation phase; your chest and shoulders feel less rigidly held; your arms feel light. Your movements are no longer jagged and hard. You end up brushing your teeth but the pressure is off. In its place is an ease of movement. You can feel it in the smoothness and openness of your energy flow. You've changed your movement print.

Chewing Your Food

Another way to take your movement pulse is by noticing how you're eating, specifically, how you're working your lower jaw in chewing.

Chewing involves opening and closing movements. When you close down on some food (really, close up on it), your teeth come together. But with how much effort? Are you assaulting the food with your teeth? Are you whacking away at it unnecessarily?

The next time you eat, try chewing with just a little less effort. Is the chewing still effective?

Try biting down (again, more exactly, biting up) with still less force. Are you still successful in breaking up the food?

Now let your lower jaw come up with the minimal force necessary to chewing the food—the least possible effort—just enough to grind what's in your mouth and not a fraction more.

You might find yourself chewing more slowly and more carefully, not because you're trying to chew more slowly or trying to chew more carefully, but because you're listening to the movement and realizing that all that upward force isn't necessary. You're realizing you don't have to do battle with what's in your mouth—not even with a raw carrot. When people are admonished to chew more carefully or to eat more slowly, they're directed to start at the end rather than at the beginning. Speed and care are a matter of movement. To decrease speed and increase care, listen to your movement and get in touch with your movement pulse.

If you follow through on this experience, decreasing effort in the same gradual way as with toothbrushing, you'll notice again that it's possible to move with less tension, and not only do what you're doing, but do it with a newfound ease. The process of chewing, like the process of brushing, can be fluid instead of choppy and tense. And as with brushing your teeth, your whole body will feel the difference. Breathing patterns become less labored; strains in face, neck, and shoulders fade. A sense of ease and facility—and greater enjoyment—come flowing in on the crest of the movement. Even though you're crunching away, channels of movement can remain open. The pleasures of eating can be enhanced and so also can your sense of aliveness.

There are other ways of taking your movement pulse throughout the day that are as common as brushing your teeth and chewing. They're built on the same basic movement patterns. The process of brushing your teeth is a matter of "getting it and keeping it together while moving it along." It involves picking something up, then holding on to it and moving with it at the same time. The process of chewing, on the other hand, involves no holding action at all. You simply open and close upon something—over and over again till nothing's left. The basic movement patterns of each activity are common to a very large range of everyday behaviors:

Picking something up and moving it along:
    picking up a pencil and writing
    picking up groceries and carrying them into the house
    picking up a fork and eating with it
    picking up the laundry and putting it in the machine
    picking up something you dropped

Opening and closing things:
    your eyes, your mouth in talking
    boxes, books
    your hand, a jar
    doors, car hoods
    envelopes, pots
    refrigerators, coats

Actually, to pick something up and ultimately release it is to open and close, or more precisely, to close and open. Thus, everything in the first category is actually in the second category as well. When you close in on the handle of your hairbrush, for example, you do it with the intention of picking it up. Indeed, picking it up is part of the gesture of closing in on it: the movements are not really separate as when you lift something heavy—a loaded suitcase, for instance. But the reverse is not necessarily true at all. When you close in on the handle of the refrigerator, you don't pick up the refrigerator. When you slip and catch yourself on a railing or grasp for a nearby tree trunk while climbing a hill, you don't pick up the railing or the tree trunk.

Listening in on simple everyday movements you discover things you'd otherwise never know. By tinkering with them, you learn even more.

The moral?

Your movement pulse is there for the taking and your movement print is always lying about. It's a shame to let either of them go unnoticed.

Chapter 3

TRANSFORMING YOUR HABITS

Decreasing effort makes a difference. It can make a difference in the way you write, play tennis, and walk down the street. Moreover making differences has a radiating effect. Or at least the possibility of same. It depends on how far you want to travel with things.

Noticing and Making Differences in Everyday Activities

If the message seems to be: cultivate a laid-back style in brushing your teeth and chewing your food, and a new world will open before you, a slightly skewed message is coming through. The aim is not a casual lifestyle—though there's nothing wrong with that. The aim is to regenerate and even increase your vitality. It's to awaken and enhance your sense of aliveness. Casualness has nothing really basic to do with it; sensing and moving do. As pointed out in the beginning, you can begin by noticing or by making differences. Either way you can transform your habits.

Pulse-taking may seem picky, a fussing over trivia, until you realize that there are basic kinds of movement you make every day of your life. Being fundamental, these movements are done over and over again in a certain way: fluidly, rigidly, smoothly, leisurely, hastily, awkwardly, and so on. Your same movement print is on them. There may be a few variations, but in general, and especially as you get older, a particular flow of movement is yours—or rather, it is you.

Once you become aware of basic movement patterns and begin listening in on them, you'll realize how easy it is to leave other movement prints about, that is, if you want to. Once you notice how you're moving, you can begin transforming your habits. You'll see that a lighter touch is literally possible.

Giving and Receiving or Finding the Transactional Balance

What happens when you get a package from the parcel service?

Do you jerk your arms forward to take it? Do you have a tendency to grab the package? to fumble it? to drop it? Do you allow the person to give it to you?

Or suppose someone offers you a newspaper or drink of some kind on the plane. How do you receive it? Do you take it hurriedly? Do you pull it back toward you? Do you take it altogether unthinkingly?

How do you do these things?

Usually you pay attention to the thing being received, not on how you're receiving it. But there are different ways of receiving things—even cumbersome things. When you're aware of how much effort you're exerting in doing something, and when you realize you can do the same thing for less, the movement becomes—well, graceful.

Graceful?

That's a difficult word for some people. It's often connected exclusively with a feminine (or effeminate) image.

But ask yourself:

What's a successful football pass receiver if not graceful?

To be graceful is to achieve a maximum of effect with a minimum of effort. It's nothing more—and nothing less—than this.

Even a difficult-but-caught catch is gracefully received when the receiver folds himself in on the ball in such a way that his movement overcomes the fugitive movements of the ball and the two continue moving on a single line of force. The receiver is not so much pursuing the ball as continuously accommodating his movement toward it. There's no gesture that deflects his energy from this bodily process of conforming to the ball's flight, no extraneous effort that detracts from the ultimately single linear dynamic. Clearly, there's not a maximum of effort and a minimum of effect but quite the reverse: the movement is graceful.

The same is true in the martial arts—in tae kwon do, for example, when the aim is to break a piece of wood with a kick. When a student successfully places concentrated attention and all of her or his energy into her/his heel that hits a very small spot on the wood, the wood breaks. There is a minimum of effort and a maximum of effect.

Football pass receivers and martial arts aside, everyone likes his or her efforts to be rewarded. No one wants to do things that don't bring results. But that's exactly what happens when grace is lacking. Too much is going into the activity and too little is coming out in the way of positive effect.

Noticings can make differences—ones that matter.

Something similar can be said of giving. In a literal sense you're extending something of yourself: your hand. In a figurative sense, what's in your hand is also something of yourself since it's connected to you. This means that in giving something, you let go of part of yourself. All this may seem so obvious that it needs no spelling out at all. But there's a point that's not obvious: giving is a doubly dynamic process. It's a matter of moving something, namely, the part of you that's in transit, and a matter of diminishing support of the thing being given. There are subtleties that have to do both with movement itself and with moving something from full to zero support.

Imagine yourself giving an orange to someone, or a bag of groceries, or something heavy like a box of books. You can go all the way from thrusting the thing into his or her hands to reluctantly relinquishing it into them. How gracefully you do it depends on your sense of movement, and on your noticing differences in support, not only your own diminishing kind but the gradually increasing kind being transmitted to you through movement. In other words, you can feel both the weight of the object lighten and your movement lighten as the object passes from you to the other person.

Have you ever been in an "Oh! I thought you had it!" situation— where someone is giving something to you or you're giving something to someone and one of you thinks the other has hold, but it turns out that that person doesn't have hold at all and the thing drops? Alas!

Noticing can make a difference—a difference that matters, even that matters to the transported matter itself.

(Ponderabilia 5: Common Misunderstandings of Movement That Occlude Its Qualitative Realities)

Turning and Touching

Consider another basic movement pattern: turning things on, off, and just plain turning:

You turn on lights

You turn off the DVD

You turn the key in the lock

You turn the pancakes over

You turn on the water faucet

You turn the knob

You turn your chair

You turn in your chair

You turn your head

Let's start small. How about all those little motions in turning appliances on and off—a little flick of the fingers in relation to a switch or a dial?

Are you attacking the switch when you turn on the radio or the light? Are you hastening the death of the washer in your faucet when you turn off the water? This is not a commercial plug for kindness to your electrical appliances. It's a question of the quality of contact with things in your everyday world. It's a question of touch.

Touch is a barometer of movement. The greater the pressure on things, the less fluid the movement with them. You noticed this with opening and closing movements and with picking-up-and-moving movements. When the pincer-like pressure on things is too hard, the channels of movement become jammed. Little flicking movements to turn a switch or a dial on or off are little barometers of tension.

Touching and Pushing

Larger movements with larger objects are just as telling.

How do you push a grocery cart in the supermarket, for example? Do you hold on for dear life? Does push come to shove? If so, it's likely that your efforts are far short of being rewarded. Unless you've had the misfortune to get a cart with a wheel that rolls perpendicular to the direction in which you're traveling—in which case the best move is to get another cart—or unless you have fifty pounds of groceries in the cart, driving the thing tank-like down the aisles is simply not necessary. And even at fifty pounds, it's probable that a lighter touch would make the pushing less arduous since more muscle power would be going into a forward motion than into a metal bar.

In short, your grocery cart is an extension of you. You're merely passing your energy on to it. If your movement isn't smooth and easy, you're working too hard. You can move through a supermarket like the man on the flying trapeze.

In fact, even if you're in a hurry you can push your way about with the greatest of ease. Heavy-handed tactics only make for heavy-footed gaits. Would you be moving as you're moving if you were hurriedly pushing a baby in a stroller instead of your groceries in a cart? Instead of digging into the floor and scissoring your legs with martial precision and stiffness, you could be gliding over it, going this way and that and feeling as if you were barely touching the ground. All it takes is a softening of pressure. The softening softens the effort of pushing. You can scurry about with your cart with enviable fleetness. Hurrying along with a light touch and a light step is literally possible.

Touch is indeed a barometer of movement. A little pressure pushes things a long way. Too much pressure doesn't really push things along at all. It just spreads out in all directions and inflates everything with tension.

Pushing and Pulling

Pulling and pushing are opposite basic movements. There's no common everyday opposite of supermarket grocery-cart-pushing, however, unless taking your dog for walks means constantly tugging at him or her. Pulling drawers and doors open is common enough, but neither is really a full-bodied action like grocery-cart pushing. So let's go back to food—not chewing it, but readying yourself for eating it.

Although there are individual styles of pulling a chair up to the table, two things are always true, and true whether you're almost seated, and then pull up your chair at the last second before you and your chair bottom meet, or whether you're already seated, in which case you lift your bottom and then pull up the chair to be closer to the table: 1) you can't pull the chair forward while sitting on it, and 2) you can't do anything but a half-squat while you're pulling it up.

How can you possibly get this act together with a minimum of effort and a maximum of effect? How can this movement be anything other than jagged and awkward? Whatever the effort expended, alas! It all seems necessary.

But here too there are tricks to be mastered—three of them to be exact. And they're not so much tricks as self-insights.

There's first of all your grip on the chair. Nine times out of ten, the chair you want closer to the table doesn't weigh very much, so why grasp it as if it were a dead weight, or even had to be first uprooted from the floor before you could move it? The first thing is to notice your grip.

Second, the half-squat in which you find yourself may seem difficult to support, but it's not at all impossible to live with gracefully once you realize it involves a rocking motion—a forward and backward rolling on your bottom or feet (depending on whether you're already or almost seated). The rocking motion allows you to pull up your chair and then sit down on it. Rocking forward allows the chair to come up beneath you as you pull it forward; rocking backward allows you to come down on the chair. Simple. The second thing then is to listen in on how you're getting into and out of your half-squat. Third, there's the pulling itself: is it an easy forward movement of the arms or is it a jerky pull that yanks the chair forward? If you've listened carefully to your body during the previous two movements, you'll find it almost impossible to jerk or yank. Jerking and yanking don't happen easily with a light grip; and they can barely happen at all with a smooth rocking motion.

Finding the key to a lighter touch and to a sense of pleasure in your own grace is there for the noticing.

Putting Your Not-So-Best Foot Forward

So far we've emphasized the noticing or listening side of sensing/moving differences. How about surprising yourself on the other side?

You're standing on a street corner waiting for the light to change. You're busy wondering whether there's a line at the bank, what the jeweler's going to charge to repair your watch, or whether they'll have the tape you want at the store. Or maybe you're just daydreaming.

Normally, you'd not give a second thought to how you're going to move when the light changes. But today, you're going to shift gears:

Think—but without actually moving—how you're going to start out when the light changes. What do you feel on the verge of doing? How do you ready yourself for moving on?

More than likely, you start out with a favorite leg. What you feel on the verge of doing, then, is shifting your weight to the non-favorite leg to free the favorite one. And you feel yourself as well on the verge of lifting your lead leg in order to swing it forward.

For a whole day, every time you're momentarily stopped—for a stoplight or whatever—every time you're going to start out anew, start with that other leg; start out by putting number two forward.

The change may feel queer at first, almost to the point that you think you've never moved that other leg before in that way. But the only thing that's really different is a new beginning. It's not as if you've grown a third leg. It's the same old one that's always been there, but, like a stepchild Cinderella, it's never been given anything close to full and favored privileges before. You're now striding forth in a new way. You've surprised yourself in movement.

On Upward Mobility

Everybody has an uphill climb at some point in their everyday lives. Surely there's an incline or upstairs someplace in your neighborhood. Even public transportation requires a step or two up. If nothing else, there is at least a curb nearby. And of course once you've stepped down onto the street, you've got to come back up again in order to continue on your way.

There are different ways of going up, just as there are different ways of giving and receiving or pulling your chair up to the table. Surprise yourself on your next uphill climb by keeping your knees slightly flexed instead of straightening them at the end of every step. You'll be making your way upward, but getting there at half the cost. The movement will feel different, too. It will feel smooth and pleasurable and will lose the start/stop or even jerky rhythm it had.

What's happened? How have you transformed your habitual upward movement? *(Ponderabilia 6: Kinesthetic Memory)*

If you notice people going upstairs or climbing up a hill, you can see them continuously flexing and extending their knees. You can see their knees go down and then up with each step. Going down means the knee of their forward leg is flexed. Going up means that their forward leg is assuming the weight and they are coming up to full height on it.

The question is whether the full extension of the supporting leg is necessary. You have to go down to go up, but do you have to go up, fully up, to make your way to the top?

The answer is "No!"

The trick to an easier feeling climb may seem to be in extending yourself fully on your supporting leg. Slow-paced climbs are often like this. You see people take a step forward, and then extend their leg fully. You even see them at times take a momentary rest at their normal height. The process often looks painful—perhaps as painful, or at least as unpleasurable, as it feels.

When you keep your knees slightly flexed so that they're always bent to some small degree—a little like Groucho Marx—your movement flows continuously forward. In consequence, your energy isn't at cross purposes with itself. In other words, you're not using nearly so much energy as you go upward because you yourself are not moving up with each and every step—and you're not actually moving that much further down either. What you really want to do when you're going upstairs or are on an uphill climb is to go forward. The fact that forward happens to lie on an upward slant or entails stepping up onto a different level shouldn't trick you into a wasted visibility. Surprise yourself by keeping a relatively low profile. And notice how pleasurable and virtually effortless your movement feels.

Of course you may still get tired on an uphill climb. If so, there's no reason why, after keeping a low profile, you can't come up, all the way up, pause, and take in the view from this greater height.

On Settling Down

You're about to sit down in your favorite reading or TV chair. You're facing the chair. You're about to turn around and sit down in it.

Which way are you turning? If your left foot's forward, you're turning right; if your right's forward, you're turning left.

Which way do you usually turn? Is turning in one direction as fluid as in the other? Or are you surprised by the feel of the movement in the reverse direction?

Whichever direction your turn, how exactly do you manage it? Do you do it in one step? in two? in three? How do you arrange your feet in the process? Do you turn them inward or outward?

If you've ever seen a cat "kneading" a spot with its paws and claws before settling down on it, the scene might recall the maneuvering that sometimes goes on when you turn before you sit. Sometimes you make elaborate preparations—all the more so if you're carrying something that needs attention, such as a cup of hot coffee. You take a number of steps to station yourself just so, and perhaps even take a sidelong over-the-shoulder, assess-the-distance glance behind you prior to coming in for a landing.

Next time you're about to sit, notice what advance arrangements you're making. Then during the whole of the day, each time you're about to sit down, mix things up a bit: the inwards and the outwards, and the number of steps; and then too, reverse the direction of your turn.

When you barge in on your habits in this good-humored, inquiring way, you become aware of what you're doing in a movement sense. You become aware of exactly what is involved dynamically in all these habits. Were you actually aware that in order to sit down, you have to do a 180-degree about-face in relation to the chair of your choice? Or did you surprise yourself? If you did, then what was in the background has shifted to the foreground. You've just given the process of settling down star billing.

When you surprise yourself in everyday happenings you throw a few new curves into your movement. The curves may seem small right now. And in fact we're beginning with small surprises. But like movement itself, surprises don't have to be big to be downright enlivening.

Putting Your Foot Down

One last surprise.

You're walking down the street, or down a very long corridor, or along the beach. You're walking somewhere where there's a lengthy open stretch before you.

You're walking along in your usual stride. An even, ongoing rhythm is apparent. You can feel it.

What happens if you step out with a slightly longer stride every third step? With this simple variation, you break into the evenness. Where before there was virtually no difference between right and left, there's now a distinctive difference. Varying every third step puts you in a new rhythmic pattern: short-short-long, short-short-long. In fact what you feel in this new rhythmic pattern is a grouping of strides. Your steps come in packages of three. Not only this but the long step is now on the right, now on the left, now on the right, now on the left, and so on. You're putting your foot down, but making differences in the process. With just this slight modification in your usual walking habit, you've created a new dynamic happening. A sense of aliveness is awakened. Walking no longer gets you simply from here to there. Walking becomes a genuinely moving experience that's fun and invigorating, and that can even keep you on your toes.

Chapter 4

MAXIMIZING YOUR AWARENESS OF AND CAPACITY FOR MOVEMENT

Here are some common, everyday situations that are overflowing with movement possibilities.
Explore! Innovate! Enjoy!

Passive Movement: Going With the Forces That Be

If your bathtub is long enough, you can stretch out your legs. If you don't hold them down, they'll float to the top. You won't have to do a thing. It's as if you were vacationing at the Great Salt Lake and went out to test the water; your legs move up all by themselves and stay suspended.

It's fun to discover your floatability. It feels good to be moved by something else in this easy, literally fluid way. All you're doing is being there. But it's the manner of your being there that makes the difference. There's not any armor between you and what's happening to you. Movement is flowing through you. You can feel it. If you're open to listening, you can hear subtleties you never heard before.

When you're riding on a bus or in a car or on a plane, there's ample opportunity for passive movement. You get jiggled this way and that;

you feel yourself leaning, swaying, or being jostled. When the vehicle turns, it's as if something's tugging you from one side to the other. If there's an unexpected swerve or stop or (in a plane) drop, you're thrown or jarred momentarily. But if your channels of movement are open, the jolting movement passes through you. It doesn't jar you into a rigidity that tries to intercept and stop the jolt. You're not gripping or resisting, but going with the force—not to the point that you're crumpling over in your seat (though this too is a possibility, of course), only to the point that you're letting the movement happen to you. You're listening to it as it goes by rather than trying to capture it and in the end squelch it inside you.

When you're open to outside movement forces, you can ride them like a wave. In fact that's another water ride you can take. Riding the waves and floating are both dynamic happenings in which you don't do any work at all. In the one, you lie back and watch the world go by; in the other, you let yourself be lifted and released over and over again. There's a buoyant sense of aliveness in this kind of passive movement. It's not an exuberant buoyancy, but it's regenerative and obviously refreshing.

Feelings of aliveness can be a pure gift when they come by way of these outside wavelengths. All you have to do is sit back and listen; the dynamics are ready-made.

There are natural movements you can ride like a wave as well. One of these accompanies you wherever you go. It requires absolutely nothing of you; it can "do you" like an outside force. When you let it happen to you, it takes on a totally different quality.

Most of the time you're not aware of your breathing. If you had to be concerned with it, you'd have no time for anything else. When you listen to yourself breathing as a dynamic happening that's happening to you, something changes. You feel yourself floating on top of the movement—going wherever it takes you, the kinetic bellows rising and falling, expanding and receding as the air fills you up then flows outward. It's like dancing and feeling the form moving through you rather than your moving through the form. You might even feel that the air is breathing you rather than you breathing the air: it breathes you out and then back. Either way, you're riding your breath like a wave and enjoying the free movement ride. It's nice to be alive on the crest of such easy movement. It's like being company and having everything handed to you instead of having to go into the kitchen and get it yourself.

Extended Movement Sequences

Everybody makes a bed at some time. Making a bed or changing the sheets involves walking, bending, lifting, pulling, plumping, smoothing, wafting, placing, folding, and much more. It's a complicated process from the viewpoint of movement. Not that the movement is difficult, but there's a lot of it—and a good deal of variety as well. What's more, the process goes on for some time. You can't go "Presto!" and then and there find your bed made.

Extended movement sequences such as bed-making and sheet-changing call out for some creative spark, some inventiveness. Making a bed can be tedious if done every day of your life in the very same way. Moreover to repeat the same movements every day without any variation is a waste of energy. With a little ingenuity, you could liven things up. You could use the same amount of energy and come up with a bit of theater or a new game plan every day.

For example, consider the possibility of certain styles of moving. You can make your bed pompously, moving about with great decorum, as if your bed—whether queen-sized or king-sized or neither—were the resting place of royalty. The dignified and deliberate style of movement that goes with this kind of bed-making is not difficult to imitate—thanks to Hollywood films and TV series. Of course if you really were a royal personage, you wouldn't be making your own bed, but that's beside the point. What matters is that you're injecting a new spark into an otherwise dull activity and livening yourself up in the process.

What happens when you move with great decorum? Well, it's not just that you don't rush about but move instead at a slow and steady pace. It's that the postural attitude of your body changes. There's an upward flow of energy. You carry your head high, so high perhaps that your neck feels like it has a giraffe-like quality. And your walk is not only slow and steady, but your leg swings and foot placements are regal, precise and measured. Your movement flows forth evenly and unperturbed—even when you catch sight of a slipper sticking out from underneath the bed. You simply flick your foot and away it goes.

You can also make GENEROUS, LARGE sheet-changing movements. When you waft a newly-opened sheet over the bed, you can waft for all you're worth. When you do, you feel the airiness of the movement ripple through you. That generous billowing up and down motion makes its way through your entire upper torso. The largeness of the movement can be a largeness not only of usually moving parts but of not usually moving parts. In fact, generous wafting or bending or lifting or plumping—generous any movements—are best if your whole body gets into the act. You can take GIANT strides, for instance, in walking movements around the bed. You can lift your legs and stretch them forth in great gulping steps. You can move your arms in LARGE swing-walking movements too. You can also re-route them by bringing them around overhead—the right arm with the left leg, the left arm with the right leg—as if you were swimming with them in the vertical, and letting them gulp space too.

What happens when you open yourself up in this generous way? You feel invigorated, unfettered, expansive—and full of movement possibilities. You're on a roll of movement inventions you never dreamed of. Creative dynamics pop out of your moving body right there on the spot. What's more, when you make differences and surprise yourself in this way, hard places soften, nodules of tension disappear. In fact your jaw may drop not just because you're surprised, but because you're relieved!

There's also the possibility of making your bed instructively, that is, making each movement a little gem of efficiency, all the while explaining to an invisible class what you're doing and how you're doing it. Maybe you're giving a running commentary to tourists who are on a tour of your home. In this case, you could point out the vintage of the bed you're making and something of its construction to your gathered listeners, all the while moving through the task at hand like a whiz, tucking and smoothing deftly like the expert you are. You could also explain to them how your methods have changed since you first learned to make a bed and how they might change in the future. A little demonstration of the differences in your polish and proficiency would not be amiss.

You might also take a holiday from the tourists and simply alternate the way in which you move as you proceed through the various steps of bed-making. You might decide to move through the first sequence slowly, the next one quickly, the next one slowly, and so on. In other words, whatever you do first—say, draw the covers back off the bed— you do it slowly, very slowly, as if you were trying to sneak the covers off the bed without its noticing. You do the next sequence quickly, smoothing the sheet and adjusting its corners as if you were keeping up with "The Flight of the Bumble Bee." When you've finished with this incredibly fast-paced smoothing and adjusting, you return to your s-l-o-w-m-o-t-i-o-n crawl, ministering to your bed with all the sprint and dash of a snail.

There are other everyday extended movement sequences that are ripe for maximizing your awareness of movement and capacity for movement. How do you go about drying yourself after a shower or bath, for instance?

You do a lot of rubbing and patting all over. You bend. You stretch. You put first one foot and then the other on the side of the tub to dry your legs. All these movements can be varied. You can take a few turns and make a few flourishes with your towel, for example. You can change the order of your rubbings and pattings, bendings and stretchings. You can play choreographer and revamp the whole. You can stamp the practical with a bit of individuality and have fun in the process.

Let's say you've just stepped out of the shower and grabbed your towel. You hold it lengthwise between your two hands and, like a matador, make a pass with it to the right, only instead of letting the movement end with your arms stretched out to one side—the towel dragging on the floor, and you on the verge of turning away from the tub as if you've just subdued it like a bull—you bring the arm that crosses your body in a circular movement overhead, and let it continue on in back of your head and out to the opposite side.

You probably do a movement similar to this in getting your towel behind you to dry your back. What's different here is the beginning matador-like pass you make with the towel and the fluid way in which it flows into the circular overhead movement. The movement gets you into your usual back-drying position, but with a distinct qualitative difference. You begin the sequence not just any old way, but with a kinetic flourish all your own.

You might think that in extending a movement sequence in this way, there's more effort, and the end result is not enhanced at all. In other words, by previous definition, the movement isn't graceful. Not only this, but you might think you're wasting your time and energy: you take a shower, dry yourself, and get on with living.

But wait before you rush away with such thoughts. Practicalities are practicalities, but gracefulness and play can enter into them.

Practicalities can be individualized as noted. They can also be pleasurable and fun. The flourishes that make them so are ipso facto worthwhile. Such flourishes take the usual mindless rush out of practical movement and bring you to immediate life. They put you in the now. They thus pay for themselves twofold: they give you an immediate sense of aliveness and give an otherwise aesthetically or creatively formless and probably thoughtless process a singular dynamic wholeness. A little flourish here, a little flourish there, and voilà! Drying yourself with a towel after a shower or bath is transformed from a dull habit into a lively experience. You not only get dried, you get dried in style. A maximum of effect is achieved and with a minimum of effort.

There used to be a test for creativity that included the question, "What are all the things you can think of to do with a paper clip?" Some of the possibilities were straightforward: use it as a tie clip; get more clips and make a necklace. Some of the possibilities were humorous: make a playground slide for ants.

Now one of the remarkable things about paper clips is that they're manipulable. You can bend them this way and that; you can attach them in interesting ways with other paper clips; you can also attach them in interesting ways to other objects. Moreover they're easily manipulable; and they're accessible in the sense that you come by them quite readily.

Oddly enough, the same can be said of movement. You can bend it this way and that; you can attach one movement to another in interesting ways; you can attach movement to objects in interesting ways. Movement too is easily manipulable, and of course everyone comes by it quite readily.

Think of an extended movement sequence as you would a paper clip—or clips. One quite movable towel and one even moderately movable body, for example, are a potent source of dynamic happenings. Explore possibilities! Let your imagination loose! You'll find that movement comes in a variety of rhythms, speeds, sizes, and shapes, and that it can oftentimes be punctuated by peels of laughter. *(Ponderabilia 7: The Gift of Play)*

48

Keeping Your Feet and More on the Ground

To maximize your awareness of movement and your capacity for movement, it's helpful to rid yourself of encumbrances: like your shoes and socks.

You probably don't think much of your toes or even think much about them. When is the last time you showered them with attention? When is the last time you took them for a walk?

Well, toes too have a right to breathe. So do feet generally of course. In fact, quite on their own, toes and feet actually move! Encased in mummy-like wrappers every day, however, and then fitted with armor besides, they're hardly in a position to move at all. Their fate is an enslavement. They're like those rows of men in the bowels of the ship who heave-ho on the oars so that the ship moves. Somebody even stands over them to make sure they do their job.

And oh! What a lowly job! But oh! too, how crucial to moving things along! Toes and feet work like mad all day. Yet what do they get for their labor? How long would you stand for such treatment? It's a wonder they don't rise up and revolt.

What would it be like to let them have the upper hand for a change?

A small breath of fresh air would be nice—a little movement or two would be very much appreciated.

Moving your toes and feet brings them to life. It brings you to life. In fact you get an altogether new lease on life where before, because of the wrappings and the armor, you couldn't even get a real live toe through the door.

If you think about it, there's no absolute and incontestable reason to wear shoes in a house. Unless your arches need constant support (in which case you might remember anyway that movement can be strengthening), or unless your floors are infested with cockroaches and vermin, shoes are encumbering. They stand between you and the world. They are interlopers of the first order. Besides, you might be surprised at how much cleaner your floors and carpets remain when they're treated to the tender, loving care that only a sensitive bare foot can give.

When you're barefoot, you not only feel things with your feet— different textures, different surface temperatures—you feel your feet! They bend! They extend! They don't do anything that would cause you the least embarrassment. Their behavior is exemplary. They are flexible and they are sensitive. As if this weren't enough, they offer a full gamut of lively possibilities—more than you might at first expect. If you liberate them from their servitude, you'll be surprised how versatile they are, and how infectious their aliveness is.

Standing on your own feet is something you can enjoy at any time during the day. Of course your feet will probably walk away with you. But don't hold back: a breath of fresh air now and then is good for everybody, and you'll enjoy the ride.

In the same way you give your feet and toes a breath of fresh air by removing the wrapping and armor, so you can give your whole body a breath of fresh air by removing it from the three-sided box you so often put it in. Think, for example, how many hours of the day are consumed in TV-watching, the original steady-state phenomenon.

You're sitting in a chair. Your hip joints are flexed. Your lower legs are hanging down. Your arm moves to reach for a snack. Your jaw moves to grind it to pieces. Then everything is pretty much quiet as before—especially your bottom half. Only your eyes are on the move.

What's interesting is that you can still see the screen, you can still take in everything when you sit on the floor. Quite apart from being better for your circulation, you give yourself some options when you're on the floor. You're not locked in on three sides. You can choose how you want to sit, and you can vary your position anytime you want: you can move.

But maybe you're thinking: I'm tired, I don't want to move. I just want to sit here and relax and be entertained.

Having some choice in the way you sit is relaxing precisely because holding yourself in the same sitting position for lengthy periods of time with your legs dangling below is not healthful for anybody's body. Bodies weren't designed for steady-state, non-stop-sitting.

Having a choice of resting—not sitting—positions isn't a commitment to manic activity. It's not a matter of constantly shifting about or thinking, "Oops! It's time for a change of position!" as if you were on a schedule. You don't have to interrupt your attention and fidget about such that you miss the program. It's simply that if you're in a chair—even a plushy, comfy, sink-to-the-bottom chair—your body movement—whatever there's left of it—will adjust itself to the limits of your settled-in state. If the chair doesn't allow you to move about easily and with some sense of freedom, then you won't move about easily with some sense of freedom. If you give yourself more space—well, you'd be surprised at what your body does with more space, or what it might do once it gets used to it.

You might, for example, find yourself sitting on the floor with your legs folded to one side or the other, your weight resting mainly on the outer side of one of your legs. You might in turn spread your arms in back and on either side of you, and by resting part of your weight on each hand as well, make yourself into a tripod.

You might sit in a tailor squat or in a lotus position, or in the position described above, but with your flexed, non-supporting leg in a vertical alignment, that is, with the knee pointing upward and the flat of your foot on the floor. You might give that knee a hug by wrapping your arms around it. You might give both knees a hug by sitting on your seat, pointing both knees upward and planting both feet on the floor.

Once down on the floor, you can stretch, fold, and balance your way through thick and thin and discover new resting places on your body in the process. But note again: you don't have to busy yourself with moving at all. Movement will come naturally on its own because you're not crammed into or cramped by a chair. This isn't to say that chairs are bad, but only that for naturally moving bodies, prolonged sits are to be avoided.

There's a final possible adventure to the story of keeping your feet and more on the ground.

Sometimes it's nice to stretch out on the floor. Not just lie down, but really stretch out. Sometimes you can look at an expanse of floor and your whole body will—well, remember what it's like when your mouth waters when you're hungry and you see something you really like—your whole body will tingle in anticipation. Stretching out in that expanse looks so inviting. It's difficult to refuse such an open invitation.

Actually, the anticipation is not so bizarre. When you think of going to the beach and utterly relaxing on the warm, firm-yet-soft, smooth-yet-hollowable surface, and letting the fresh smell and sound of the ocean waft you into a kind of semi-sleep, you think of stretching out in a somewhat similar way. What you don't get on the floor of your living room is the warmth of the sun, the moldable surface, the fresh sea smell and the sound of the breaking waves. That's quite a lot you don't get. But then you don't get sand in your ears either.

Very often surrounds are cluttered and don't invite you to stretch out, much less move. But stretching out on the floor in your own house can be rejuvenating, especially if you're not wedged between the bed and the bureau, or if you don't have to tuck your head underneath the coffee table. If you're lucky enough to have a genuine expanse, enough space so you don't feel hemmed in when you stretch to the fullest, you can explore a whole range of stretches: straight ones, twisted ones, side ones, on-your-back ones, and more. You can combine stretches and be off in a number of different directions at once—or in a number of different directions sequentially if you're so inclined. For instance, lying on your back, you might start out by stretching out in all directions, then, lifting one leg gently off the floor and just high enough to clear the other one, let it pass across the still leg and continue on, reaching out with it into the uninhabited space at your side. Let your toes lead the way by pointing in the direction you're traveling. And keep going. Find out where any stretch will take you. One part of you after the next will follow along.

Stretching movements are revitalizing. Even rolling from one end of the room to the other—and rolling can incorporate stretching—is revitalizing. It feels good to come down to earth in the form of a floor. Of course if you're at a picnic or in your backyard and have an expanse of grass to roll or stretch out on, you're in luck too. The point is that flat on your back, or flat on your side, or twisted, or rolling, you're not relinquishing your dignity, but restoring and reinvigorating it. You're following your creative stretches, twists, rolls, and more wherever they lead.

Where Is the Movement Coming From? Reaching Arms, Walking Legs, Standing and Sitting (or Rocking and Jumping)

Reaching Arms

When you want the salt shaker, you reach for it; when you want to embrace another person, you reach out to them; when you drop your book on the floor, you reach to pick it up.

Arms are wonderfully handy. Hands, by definition, are even handier. But the handiness of arms shouldn't be overlooked on that account.

Arms come in two fairly equal pieces. When you reach for something you almost invariably extend your arm at the elbow joint. When you become aware of the commonness of this movement, you'll appreciate how basic it is to your very survival. If you've ever had a cast on your favorite arm, you'll already know how impossibly restricted you are when you can't extend it from the elbow. You're virtually helpless to minister to yourself: combing your hair, brushing your teeth—to say nothing of eating—become temporarily lost arts.

Now very often when you reach for something, you first need to lift your arm. You have to get it out of neutral, that is, move it from its normal dangling position at your side. The question is, what do you do when you lift your arm? Do you lift it all in one piece?

The answer is probably "Yes."

When you lift your arm in this way, you're moving your whole arm from the shoulder joint. You're picking the whole thing up in one fell swoop. This is what usually happens even when your arm is not in neutral—when it's resting on your lap, for instance, before you reach for the salt. In other words, even if your elbow is somewhat bent, you tend to lift your whole arm at once.

Of course you don't have to lift your arm in this way. There's no law that says, "All arms to be lifted from the shoulder joint only."

Well, then, what are the alternatives?

There are basically two of them: you can lift your arm from the elbow, or you can lift your arm from the wrist.

The next time you're going to reach for something on the top shelf, let the movement come from your wrist: lift it, and let it lead the way. You'll find your whole arm following it upward. It has nowhere else to go. Your fingers will follow it upward too if you let them. Only when you reach your destination at the top is it time for them to carry their own weight and finish off the movement by reaching for whatever it is you've come for. *(Ponderabilia 8: On Creativity, Wonder, and the Unsung Kinetic Imagination)*

You might do this movement several times over to get the literal hang of it. Arm and fingers are dragged along by an upwardly mobile wrist. The wrist is their leader until the very end. Don't empower other parts along the way!

Of course you can't move your whole arm without involving your shoulder joint. But you feel the movement dominated by your wrist, just as you would feel it dominated by your elbow if it led the way—speaking of which:

The next time you're lying in bed and about to reach over and turn off the light, initiate the movement from your elbow. Begin by moving it to the side away from your body. As it moves away from you in the direction of the nightstand, it pulls the whole of your arm along with it in the same direction. When it's gone as far as it can go, let the lower arm take up the movement: continue in the same direction by extending your forearm. Though your elbow's no longer in the lead, you can feel the movement at the elbow. The two pieces of your arm open up more and more until they form a straight line—at which point, Presto! You've arrived at the light switch, but this time with a creative flair.

If you picture someone gesturing as he or she says, "Give me some elbow room!" you'll have a general image of what it means to focus movement at the elbow. Actually, elbows are fairly stationary in a give-me-some-elbow-room gesture. It's by dint of movement at your shoulder joints that you have moving elbow room on both sides. But you feel the gesture at the elbow all the same.

You might like to give yourself some doubly-full elbow room, whether you're lying down or standing up. All you need is full-arm space on either side of you. Instead of moving your elbows out and back, and out and back several times over as in your usual bent-at-the-elbow "give me some elbow room" gesture, let them lead outward as usual, and then, instead of bringing them in, let both continue as in the full arm extension "light switch" movement described above. When you have all the elbow room your elbow joints are capable of giving you, you'll be ready to embrace the world, or anyone you like who comes your way. Your chest is open. Your reach is wide and full. Your breath is unobstructed. You feel expansive. There's a breadth to your being—and a generous sense of aliveness.

Walking Legs

In the same way you can lift and extend your arms in different ways and feel new dimensions open up, so you can lift and extend your legs and feel new dimensions too. This lifting and extending of legs is not a strange or complex movement pattern at all. It's called walking.

Where does the movement come from when you walk? Where do you initiate the forward-striding action of each leg?

If you listen carefully, you can feel the lift from your hip joint—first the left one, then the right. The hip joints, by the way, are not those prominent bones you can feel with your fingers several inches below your waist. Like all joints, the hip joint is not a bone, but the site of an articulation of bones. The easiest way to find your hip joint is to begin bringing your knee to your chest. The closer your knee comes toward your chest, the deeper the crease—or angle—between your torso and leg. Your hip joint is at the crease. It allows the interplay of movement between your legs and torso. It allows you to bend your torso over your legs—as when you bend over to pick something up—and to lift and extend your leg forward and upward toward your torso—as when you kick something away from you.

Now suppose that instead of walking from the kitchen to the bedroom in regular fashion—or if you're daring, from your office desk to the drinking fountain—you extend the lift period of your walk. The lift period is not something you can watch, at least not easily. It's something you do behind your back. You've probably never given it much thought before, but the leg you lift in walking is always the leg you've left behind. To extend the lift period of your walk, lift your back leg a little higher than usual and keep it there for a little longer time than usual as well.

Normally, as your toe loses contact with the ground, you lift your leg by bringing your knee forward and flexing at the hip joint. What you're doing now is lifting your leg from the hip joint as your toe loses contact, and extending your hip joint in the process.

Obviously you'll not arrive at your destination as quickly. But you'll certainly enjoy the trip there as never before. For one thing, you feel your hip joints getting a bit of fresh air; you feel their openness. You don't have to lift your leg high in back to feel the openness. Just slightly higher than in normal walking.

Perhaps one reason the openness feels so good—and different—is that it's such a contrast to the minimal movement we offer our hip joints. When you're sitting, your hip joints are closed; there's no way of getting through to them. They're buried in that crease we spoke about earlier. If hip joints were places of business, they'd right away go broke because of being closed most of the day.

Open-hip-joint walking doesn't just give hip joints a chance to breathe; it also involves a change of pace. It's not just that the movement is slower; the whole rhythm of walking changes. The way in which it changes depends on how you're coordinating the supporting action of one leg with the lifting action of the other. In fact, it's possible that you've discovered a natural swinging rhythm in the movement of the free leg: if after you lift your leg backward, you let it swing forward instead of carrying it forward, you discover that instead of stepping onto the front leg and then lifting the one in back, you're lifting the back one as you step onto the front one. The backward lift in this swinging walk is like the preparatory backswing you take prior to kicking something. It's a quite natural movement. (Try kicking something—a ball or wadded-up piece of newspaper—to recall this once-familiar movement if you happen to have forgotten it.)

What's nice about a swinging walk is precisely its swinging quality. Swings feel very good. When you really swing something, its weightiness disappears. You let its built-in momentum carry it along. In addition, movement and breath cadences coincide exactly with one another. You can literally feel yourself breathing the movement's rhythm. A minimum of effort and a maximum of effect is very much in evidence.

Now it's not just that movement doesn't happen except for the having of joints. It's that movement is good for joints. That's what they were designed for. Joints don't simply allow the maintenance of a variety of positions. They are the means whereby one position after the other is achieved. In the process, they open parts of us up and close parts of us off; they turn parts of us this way and that. They enable us to move. When we move, we allow them to articulate. It's a mutually satisfying process.

When we don't move, joints give up on us. When we don't move, joints tend to get set in their ways—the ways in which we've last left them.

Standing and Sitting (or Rocking and Jumping)

Can you imagine what it would be like not to be able to sit down if you were standing, or not be able to stand up if you were sitting? Moving up and down along a vertical axis is basic to human life. We come up

60

to standing and ease ourselves down to sitting many times over in the course of a day. The question is, where do you start moving when you begin sitting or standing? It's obvious the movements are coming from the articulation of some joints, but where? Which ones? Before trying to answer the question, surprise yourself by transforming some habits.

You're sitting in a chair. You forgot to bring something with you—your book, your coffee, the newspaper, or the telephone. You need to get up and get it, and then you want to come back and sit down. Simple, yes? But instead of just getting up . . .

Suppose you start by picking up both feet from the floor. When you pick them up and listen carefully, you feel movement in your lower back and hip joints. You have a tendency to rock backward just a bit on your seat. Depending on your chair and the way you're sitting on it, your torso and head tend to tilt backward too as you lift your feet.

Suppose you give in to that tilt. Suppose you lift your feet from the floor and as you do so, you let yourself rock backward. You might think you're further than ever from standing up and getting that book, coffee, newspaper, or telephone. But now let yourself follow through on the completion of that backward rock: rock forward, and as you do so, let your feet come back down on the floor.

Are you back at square one sitting in your chair?

Well, yes and no. You are sitting in your chair, but you're not back at square one. In rocking forward, you've generated forward momentum. The forward momentum can offer you a partially free ride to the nearest upright—supposing you care to take advantage of it.

In case you didn't feel the forward momentum, rock back and forth a few times to find it: lift your feet and let their lift tilt you backward; then rock forward and let the forward rock carry your torso forward as your feet come back to the floor.

With the next forward rock, surprise yourself by standing up.

You've gotten something for less than you thought. You've not yet gotten the thing you wanted, but you've gotten something else in the process. You've gotten a creatively exhilarating ride to the top, and you're in exactly the position you need to be in to get your book, coffee, or whatever.

A little note: if you've let your torso and head tilt downward as well as forward as you rock forward, you'll have to uncurl yourself as you stand up. In fact, the way in which you come to standing will depend upon the amplitude of the arc of your rock, where your feet are placed in relation to the chair, the chair itself, the way you're sitting in it, and many other variables. Movement is full of complexities and subtleties. That's part of its charm. Explore the complexities and subtleties. Play around with possibilities now and then during the week and find what feels like the smoothest, easiest, and freest ride to the top. Then see if and how it works when you move to another chair.

But let's return to your original chair with whatever you've gotten up for. There's the matter of sitting down in it again. You've got to get the chair's bottom and your bottom to meet. The meeting involves bending and tilting. Unfortunately, you can't rock yourself down to sitting in the same way you can rock yourself up to standing. But even though you can't rock in reverse, you can do something analogous to "rocking down." Just as you can take a preparatory backward rock from which to generate forward momentum to take you to standing, so you can take a preparatory jump from which to generate downward flexing to take you to sitting.

When you jump, you go up. But you also come down. When you come down, your knees bend quite naturally. Your ankles flex—quite naturally. Your hip joints flex—quite naturally. All you have to do is channel all of the natural flexion into sitting down. When you do, your downward flowing energy goes into the chair—smoothly, gently, and oddly enough with less feeling of effort than when you lower yourself into the chair as usual, or even flop yourself into the chair heavily or sloppily. In going down with more sequentially flowing joint articulations, the process of sitting just plain feels easier. Why? Because you're getting another partially free ride. Instead of supporting yourself every bit of the way down, you're free-floating part of the way and effortlessly gathering momentum for the rest of the trip.

A Little Investment Goes a Long Way

By making a little longer investment, you might amuse yourself for a few moments. Instead of stopping the upward momentum generated in rocking by standing, let it go into a jump. Similarly, instead of stopping the downward momentum generated in jumping by sitting, let it flow backward into a rock. Try it out cautiously, even slowly at first, to see what bodily articulations and relationships are involved. Rocking and jumping and rocking and jumping. You can't fall asleep while you're doing this because either you'll not be able to keep from laughing, or you'll not be able to keep from smiling at the wonders of movement and your aliveness.

Chapter 5

SURPRISING YOURSELF: MAKING MORE DIFFERENCES

How much movement do you want to put into your life? If you're open to exploring new spaces and to doing two things at once, you can keep yourself in surprises for as long as you like.

An impossible claim?

Not at all. Don't underestimate the power of movement or your power to move and even invent on the spot!

We'll start by describing some possible adventures in outer space and end with ways of doubling up on your accomplishments.

Adventures in Outer Space: Navigating by Feel

You may think there's not much you could have missed in the way of space since you've been moving about in it all your life. But the territory is really extensive and you can venture forth in it in so many different ways. Chances are that even with moving about in it your entire life, you haven't mapped it all.

Take the territory overhead, for example. When was the last time you were there? When was the last time you were over your head in the dark as it were, moving your arms about in the upper reaches of space but not looking at where you were going?

Whenever it was, you were doing it all by feel, an old and noble way of finding your way about. In fact, an old and noble way of knowing where you are at any moment: by feel, not look.

You know where your knees and nose and toes are right this minute, and you know their spatial relationship to one another right this minute. You know furthermore that their spatial relationship right now is different from the one when you were bending over to put on your socks. You know without looking. You know kinesthetically. The knowledge is in your bones and muscles—and in your every movement.

In fact, your kinesthetic sense never deserts you—even when you're in the dark! It doesn't even desert you when you're not moving. If it did, you'd never be able to go from zero to reaching for your glasses or getting up to fetch your keys. You'd have no idea where your hands or feet were short of looking about for them. Without an ongoing kinesthetic awareness, you'd be looking for your mouth or your leg in the same way that you sometimes look for the screwdriver or your comb—things you had just two minutes ago, but can't recollect for the life of you where you last laid them.

In the outer space odysseys that follow, the emphasis will be on recognizing spatial patterns by feel, in part because the patterns aren't visible to begin with. They're line drawings that are drawn by the body in the process of moving rather than being written in pencil or pen, and they are felt rather than seen. You can visualize the lines, but you can actually feel them in the process of drawing them. Take circles, for instance, especially since we'll be moving in them almost exclusively. When you say you're 'going in circles' you can mean it as a 'figure of movement' as well as a 'figure of speech'. What you mean is that the circles you're going in are imaginary forms strung out on movement.

Getting In Over Your Head

Going in circles as a 'figure of movement' is a never-ending way of regenerating yourself. When you go in circles, you go off the beaten path, but in such simple, easy ways of moving, you never lose your way. What a pleasure to go places where you never have to ask directions!

Going in circles and getting in over your head may sound like an extreme form of self-punishment, but actually it's a delightful and satisfying way of putting movement into your life. You need only be in a standing position or moving from one place to another with nothing in your hands—or at least nothing cumbersome in your hands.

When you're ready to go, you simply begin lifting one arm and moving it upward, fully extended in front of you. When it reaches shoulder height, let it continue climbing upward. When it reaches the top and is directly overhead, keep it going still further in a descent in back of you until it finally reaches its original starting point at your side. Once started, the movement is continuous. No stopovers. No re-routings along the way. You're going in circles and have gotten in over your head.

Try the same movement with your other arm.

Once you've gone this far, try going in more than one circle at a time. If you windmill your arms, you can go in two circles simultaneously. At any moment, your arms will be at exact opposite points in their circles: when one is in front, the other is in back; when one is up, the other is down.

You can also go in two circles at the same time by moving your arms concurrently in the same direction. Start this movement backward as well as forward. You might feel a bit as if you're swimming out of water. Let your whole upper torso get into the swim.

Whether windmilling or swimming, the feel of the movement will vary a good deal according to how quickly or slowly you're doing it. Your arms can run in circles, or they can take a leisurely stroll. Find your preferences. When you're in low gear you might try stretching and reaching your way along the circular path, savoring every moment along the way, but without stopping the flow of movement.

It's possible also of course to move in different circles at the same time by reversing the direction of one of your arms. You can do a "crawl" with one arm and a "backstroke" with the other, moving one arm backward (not from the elbow, but from the shoulder joint), then overhead, then forward and downward at the same time that you move the other arm forward, then overhead, then backward and downward. Your arms may feel as if they're passing each other in the night, a strange night at first, but as the movement becomes more familiar, you'll be sorry you didn't learn how to swim out of water years ago. It's so refreshing and refreshingly simple.

Now that you've gotten in over your head in this literally roundabout fashion, the way is clear to make a more direct exploration of the space up there.

In the course of a day, you go through many a doorway. Going from one room to another, you walk through a rectangular arch, not only in your own home, but in offices where you work, or where you're a visitor, client, or patient. Doorways can of course be wonderfully symbolic. They can be portals to worlds you never dreamed of. You can turn over a new leaf by making your way through a different door or be transformed by going through just the right door at just the right time. The doorways we're interested in might turn out to be symbolic in such ways, but at bottom, they're simply openings from one space to another.

You've probably seen old Hollywood gangster-type films where one of the heavies says to another, "Reach for it!" The person is expected to put his arms up over his head.

When you go through the doorways of your home, tell yourself to do the same. Lift your arms and "Reach for it!" every time you cross a threshold. It feels refreshing. If you pause for a moment and let the reach turn into a stretch, you will feel even more refreshed. Either way, the movement opens you up. You can't put your arms overhead and remain stooped or slouched—at least not without looking like the ogre in a child's fairy tale.

If the top of the doorframe is too high for you, don't let that deter you. "Reach for it!" anyway. What counts is the openness. What counts is the lift you give and the lift you get.

Going through doorways, you can change your life—instantaneously!

Taking the Long Way Round

We usually walk in straight lines, and we do this even though there's enough room to do otherwise: no ropes or railings box us in and prevent us from going on something other than the straight and narrow. Well then, why not break new ground?

Suppose you've just taken a shower and you're going into the kitchen to get something to drink before going to bed. Instead of walking straight into the kitchen, why not take a roundabout path? If a piece of chalk were attached to your feet, you'd leave a circular trail behind you, an arc traced out on the floor between the bathroom and the kitchen.

After getting your drink, try another roundabout to bed.

Depending on the roominess of your rooms, your roundabouts can be as large as you want to make them. They can also be compound or simple.

For example, if you've a fair amount of room to move in, you can make consecutive arcs, first in one direction, then another, something like drawing continuous S curves. You go along one curve of the consecutive arcs, then back across the center axis of the S, then around

70

the next curve, then back through the center axis once more, and so on—like a series of switch-backs up the mountain side, only curved.

If your rooms aren't this roomy, make S curves the next time you're in a space where you do have room: the city park, down your driveway, across the parking lot, even down a supermarket aisle (at unpeak hours of course). You'd be surprised at how inconspicuous your roundabouts can be when you stretch out the S curves a bit, elongating them as if they were made of rubber.

You can even S-curve your way down the street and no one will be the wiser.

Arcs come in many different shapes: S curves, domes, scallops, spirals, and more. Choose your own. Vary your choice too by changing the degree of openness and length of the arcs. With a little ingenuity, you still get from A to B, but with a new twist. Going in arcs makes for a whole new trip. It reminds you that the shortest distance is not necessarily the most interesting, satisfying, or fun way to travel between two points.

It also reminds you of how intimately connected you are—how one part of you affects all other parts. Circular movements encourage you to lean this way and that. The leanings are natural compensations. They balance you on your roundabouts: they're subtle adjustments. Once you find them you can plump them up a bit. The whole of your torso and head can get into the act, and in substantial ways. You can make differences: gigantic, king-size, large, medium, small, minute, and very subtle differences, just by leaning to this degree and that as you're wending your way along the curves.

Curving your way about as you move through the day, you'll be surprised at how enlivening movement can be, how it can plump up your spirits as well as your leanings this way and that, how it can undo nodules of tensions and regenerate a sagging energy on the spot.

Chin Up

How long has it been since you looked up at the ceiling? All the way up. Or at the sky? Not just out and up, but up—directly overhead—your forehead and chin on the same horizontal plane.

How do you get your forehead and chin on the same horizontal plane?

Not just by tilting your head backward, but by super-tilting—going beyond the normal. You overshoot the mark, and by going out of your way you arrive at a new view of the world.

Perhaps you've already noticed, and even studied, this world. Elevators are notorious places for ceiling inspectors, though not all are full-fledged masters of course. Some don't quite achieve a fully horizontal inspection. But it's here you'll find the greatest tendency toward the horizontal, especially if upwardly mobile chins are not stopped in their tracks by visual distractions en route, distractions such as flashing numbers on the dashboard above the elevator doors. If they're not deflected from their course, chins will continue a long way toward the horizontal.

Indoor house-painters have a built-in possibility if not certainty of super-tilting. You can't really be engaged in painting a ceiling without looking at it. And you can't minister to it on a ladder or assay the job you've done without at some point looking directly overhead.

Why is it nice to move your chin all the way up, to the point you're looking directly overhead?

A quippish but accurate answer might be that it's such a rare treat since you don't paint your ceilings that often. Another more proper answer might be that it's nice because it's an exaggeration of an already positive response. When you say "Yes!" and gesture with your head at the same time, your chin goes up—and down. When you move your chin up to the fullest, you're accentuating the positive. Still another proper answer might be that it's nice because it's a significant phase of a roundabout journey: head circling.

Let's consider this possibility.

When you circle your head, you start out with your chin buried in your neck. It's as down as a chin can be. It's also as double as a chin can be. When you begin rolling your head to the right, your chin runs along your collarbone toward your right shoulder. Then it begins its upward journey. It loses or begins losing all vestiges of a double. It's on its way to the top—alone.

You know you're almost there when you see the ceiling coming into full view. When you reach the full overhead view you might want to stop for a moment of contemplation. When you're ready to move on again, you continue on to the left, your overhead view now ebbing away as your chin first approaches your left shoulder, then nuzzles along the left side of your collarbone, all the while collecting its doubles again, and comes finally to rest, buried in your neck.

It's nice, of course, to make the trip several times. You go along your roundabout first in one direction a few times, then in the other a few times. Or you can alternate directions each time you start out anew.

Head circling is a marvelous way of regenerating yourself. When you listen to the movement and take in all the sights along the way, you're taking a different kind of head trip, one in which your body isn't left behind—the whole of you is invited and comes along. This is because everything is in fact connected to everything else, not mechanically, but kinesthetically. When heads roll, everything feels it. *(Ponderabilia 9: Thoughts About Space, Motors—and More!)*

That everything feels it suggests that head rolling might be particularly appropriate when you're watching TV and a commercial comes on. Going on a roundabout is a splendid way of coming back to yourself and yea-saying your own aliveness, relieving tensions and lightening a felt heaviness or tiredness in the process. It is a splendid antidote to hard- and soft-sell drivel. If enough heads were rolling, they might even make an impression.

Kicking Up Your Heels and Taking a Load Off Your Feet

You've just taken your head on a little trip. Now how about your feet? They too can be a source of revival. The problem is they can't make differences when they are weighted down. What you have to do first is sit down and take the load off your feet. Then you can take them on a trip without leaving home.

Feet have remarkable directional abilities, as you must have discovered when you were little and had to sit in chairs in which you dangled from the knees down. One of the nicest things about being little or short is sitting in chairs in which you have no choice but to dangle from the knees down. It's an open invitation to movement: nothing is in the way of making a few choice turns with your feet. Why not surprise yourself now by rediscovering their directional abilities? Quite apart from marching you now where you want to go, feet are quite capable of going off on their own without getting lost.

Going in circles without touching the ground is everyone's possibility, for example. Even old feet can be wayward every which way. And of course you don't have to be little or short to dangle. All you have to do is lift your foot off the floor and draw some circles with it, circles as large as your ankle joint will allow. If you imagine a piece of chalk at the end of your big toe, you can visualize the circles as you draw them. Go round and round first in one direction and then the other. If you hear some creaking sounds, don't be alarmed. They're only signs of a resurrected life.

Now feet are rather ingenious. They can't actually move in circles—your heels always remain in place and no insisting will change their minds—but they can make you feel as if they were moving in a circle. Such benign deceit might be more than you'd expect of feet, unless you've known them very well and have already realized how very versatile and capable they are.

There's a small, four-legged desert animal that finds respite from the hot sand by lifting its feet: it balances for a moment first on one side, then the other. The feet on each side thus have a chance to be cooled. We have neither four feet to look after nor do we have perpetually hot feet to deal with. What we do have though—like the small desert animal—is the perpetual possibility of picking up a foot—one or two at a time—and making a few choice turns with it before continuing on along our appointed rounds.

Doubling Up

Doing two things at once can be as revitalizing as exploring new spaces. In each kind of experience, it's a matter of awakening yourself to movement possibilities in the situation at hand.

On the Phone

You listen, you talk, you listen, you talk.

Maybe you're doodling at the same time. Maybe you're drumming your fingers on a table or desk. Maybe you're stuck on the phone and can't hang up but wish you could. What do you do?

You do a little toe-dance.

You rock up onto your toes by extending your ankle, then flex your ankle and return your whole foot to the floor. You can do an all-ten-toe-dance, or, if you're standing, you can shift your weight and toe-dance first on one side, then the other.

You keep following what's being said to you, but you notice too how good it feels to do a little toe-dancing on the side. You discover that once on your toes, you can peck, poke, or dab around with them. In fact, you can make imaginary designs. As you dab here, here, here, and here, you can sense the linear connection between the present point of contact and the next and the next and the next, and come up with anything from an imaginary house to an imaginary penguin in the process. It's like seeing stars in the sky as forming a constellation, or like those numbered dots on a page that make a picture of something when you connect them.

On the other hand—or foot—you might want to draw the connections themselves. You might want to doodle with your toes. You can glide your toes along the floor and draw lines from here to there to wherever. All sorts of linear patterns are possible: triangles, rectangles, spirals—a host of underfoot forms awaits your fancy. You can even intersperse some dabs with your linear patterns and do some mock toe-painting.

Doodling with your toes is the next best thing to being off the phone. Of course doodling with your toes is even better if you remove your shoes and socks. Nothing takes the place of in-person communications.

At Your Desk

You're sitting at your desk reading, your eyes and hands concentrated on some task, whether sifting through a tedious report, writing a difficult letter, or calculating your income tax.

What do you do by way of keeping your spirits alive and refreshed in such a situation? What do you do to let tensions that creep in, creep out?

You start rocking on your seat—very discreetly. You tilt your pelvis backward just a little bit so that your weight comes forward, that is, toward and over your legs; then you tilt it forward just a little bit so that your weight goes backward and away from your legs.

The small rocking motion can be felt all the way up your spine. It feels very nice. You're stretching your lower back first in one direction, then another, first arching, then rounding. The happenings up and down your back are small and subtle but they're palpably present. Not only this but they make a difference. They liven things up in just the right amount: not so much as to be distracting, but enough so that joints and vertebrae don't get too set in their ways while you're busy with your work.

The small rocking motion is nice too because it takes the pressure off. By moving things around a bit, the part on which you're sitting doesn't get tired and worn. After all, you're boring down on one spot and could eventually work your seat to the bone unless you surprise yourself now and then with a little rock forward, a little rock backward. Your income tax may still be a challenge, but in doing two things at once, you find a smooth and pleasurable counterpoint to your labor. It's like singing when you're working outside—only here, the song is sung in movement.

Of course you can rock yourself backward and forward in larger movements and increase the range of your archings and roundings. When you rock in a slow, smooth, ample way, one area after the next is awakened. You begin by feeling articulations ripple up your spine and end by feeling a resurgence of life in the whole.

After a while you may find that such rockings ought to carry a warning label: this movement could be hazardous to your work!

At the Sink

You're washing dishes, brushing your teeth, or preparing vegetables.

Whatever the task, can you give it slightly less attention? Can you let both your knees flex—not suddenly as if you're going to drop to the floor, but smoothly and slowly?

Listen to your descent. The movement doesn't have to be large any more than it has to be fast. Just an easy bending of your knees. After you've gone down a few inches, come back up again to normal standing height—again, slowly—not as if you're being shot up in the air by a rocket. And no need to lock your knees either. Keep them flexibly ready for moving.

Go down and up several times in gentle, easy flexions and extensions. You can feel the angle at your knees increase as you go down and disappear as you come up; you can feel your bottom go down toward your heels and then move away from them as it comes back up.

After you've gotten into a nice, easy rhythm going down and up and down and up, feel where your feet are in relation to one another. If they're closer together than the width of your hips, move them apart to coincide with the width of your hips. Do this without looking. See if you can do it just by feeling where your feet are and where you want them to be. And continue in your gentle, easy down-and-up rhythm.

If you've finished your chores at the sink, save the next installment for a return visit. If you're still at it, make a further difference—while continuing with the difference you've already made.

As you flex your knees, move your hips slowly to the left, as slowly as you're flexing your knees; then, as you extend your knees, move your hips slowly back to center. On your next round trip down and up, move your hips slowly to the right and then again slowly back to center. Your hips are going from side to side and your knees are going up and down. You're going in two different directions at the same time—a two-in-one surprise! Moreover depending upon whether and to what degree you're bent over the sink, the feel of the movement might reach into nooks and crannies you never knew existed before, particularly along the sides of your back and along your backside proper.

Actually, going in more than one direction at the same time isn't that uncommon. If you jog, or if you've watched joggers, you may have noticed how incredibly complicated the directional patterns are. It's almost surprising that any headway is made. Legs are making circles, one after the other. Arms are moving in the same plane as the legs, but going forward and backward. While all this is going on, the whole body is going up and down with each forward step. Round and round, forward and back, up and down. You'd think the whole thing would fall apart.

The more you're aware of directional possibilities in movement, the more you realize your capacity to surprise yourself, not just in the sense of making actual forward progress in jogging, but in the sense of discovering different ways of putting yourself together in movement: a little bend here, a little lift there, a little stretch here, a little twist there, all at the same time—and voilà! You're doing more than you dreamed possible.

A breath of fresh air comes rippling in on these discoveries. A sense of aliveness is present in the realization of how much movement there is in you, and how ever-ready it is to sing out a little and let its voice be heard. *(Ponderabilia 10: In the Beginning . . .)*

A final note: When you speed up the knee flexions and extensions, you'll find a delightful bouncy quality in the movement. Your knees will be slightly flexed at the top of the bounce instead of at a full extension each time. In effect, you'll find that the movement rebounds each time almost by itself and that it has a fluid rhythm to it besides. It's continuous instead of start/stop and in consequence less likely to be jerky.

Just because you're going faster in your flexions and extensions doesn't mean you have to throw your weight around. An easy displacement here and there will do nicely. Anything more than this is fine, but be forewarned again: this movement too may be hazardous to your work!

Occupied But Empty-Handed

Suppose you're sitting at a table after having dinner with family or friends. Suppose, in other words, you're occupied in some casual way but not doing anything with your hands. Of course you could do some toe-dancing on the floor underneath the table. No one would possibly guess you were choreographing a pas de deux for your own two feet.

But you have other options too. Your shoulders are relatively free. You can gently shrug them, for instance—slowly and without fanfare. You might even lift them and let out a little sigh as you lower them, not so loud as to be distracting, but enough to be satisfying. Lifting and lowering your shoulder feels good. It also feels quite natural and simple. You don't have to stop doing what you're doing and give them undivided attention. Just a little corner will do.

Sometimes you'll find your shoulders coming down to a lower point than the one from which they started. Sometimes you don't notice how jammed your circuits of movement are until after you've moved, and by moving, dissipated some of the tension. When you listen to movement in this way, it's much like taking your movement pulse: by making differences and noticing, you get a "before" and "after" reading. You open channels of movement that were to this moment tightly shut. Necks and shoulders are notorious places for tensions to set in, and in fact not just set in, but set up housekeeping. You don't even realize you've given them squatter's rights.

A wonderful thing about moving is that you can be aware of what's moving as well as of the movement itself. As you lift and lower your shoulders, listen to them as well as their movement. They can probably tell you quite a story.

Now if gently shrugging your shoulders feels nice, think what more than a simple shrug might feel like . . .

You can draw a few circles with your shoulders when you're listening in a casual way to something or doing some light reading, for instance. You can move them forward, up, back, and down; you can move them back, up, forward, and down. In short, you can circle them starting either forward or backward. Oddly enough, while you can probably move each one separately with ease when you start forward, when you start backward, the trip may be somewhat bumpy. Smooth it out by moving both shoulders together when you do backward-starting circles. There's something about company that makes a difference.

Shoulders can go one way, then turn around and retrace their steps, or they can continue on for a few rounds in one direction and then in the other. Whichever way you route them, the trip should be a smooth and pleasant one.

Shoulder movements are naturally discreet to begin with. Of course they can be as ruggedly independent and flamboyant as an arm or leg, a head or a hip. But when you're doing two things at once, it's best to go with their moderate nature. When you do, you'll find them marvelously adaptable. They're easy to live with alongside other activities and they blend in easily with the atmosphere. So move them gently up and down or round and round. You'll surprise your back and neck as well as your shoulders. You may in fact receive thank-you notes from all over.

Cleaning

Cleaning is a dreary-sounding subject. There's not much you can say to recommend it. Vacuuming, polishing, dusting, sweeping: the mere words are enough to turn you in the opposite direction, to the nearest door, and out of the house completely.

Can you possibly put a little movement into your cleaning life?

Is it possible for these dreary activities to find redemption in movement?

What can you do while you vacuum? Well, for openers, you can alternate between a ballerina-tippy-toe-across-stage and a Groucho-Marx-bent-knees-gulping-space-exit-walk while you're getting all those threads, pieces of lint, and unidentified fallen objects duly whooshed up and out of sight. You can carry that nozzle or hold onto that upright and all the while go from an elevated and ethereal sublime to a low wide-stepping ridiculous. You can gambol your cleaning life away in whatever movement nonsense comes to mind courtesy of your body. You'll be surprised at how zaniness drives away dreariness, turning what was drudgery into fun and what were stressful tensions into a delightful lightness of being.

You might also zigzag your way about the room as if the vacuum were leading you instead of you leading the vacuum. When you let the vacuum have its way like this, you're doing two things at once: vacuuming and practicing a bit of imaginative self-deceit in the interests of drumming up a little vitality to get yourself through the cleaning drearies and onto the other side. When you allow the vacuum star billing, you follow its every whim and defer to its peculiar habits: its idiosyncratic ways of turning, its addiction to making certain noises on picking something up it didn't like, its tendency to ignore certain unidentified fallen objects while gobbling up others. For now, you don't force it to retrace its steps. You let it take you for a ride.

When you do this, it's likely that wads of tension that have taken up residence in your body will soften, your grip will relax, your pushing this way and that will be far, far less pushy, and your steps will be lighter. Your sense of aliveness will come humming back in—even over the din of the vacuum.

At this point an unexpected change may come over you. Your attitude toward the vacuum might change. You might begin feeling a kind of respect for it. You might even ask yourself, "How would I like to grovel my way about the house like this? How would I like to keep my nose to the ground, snivelling about in this way?"

Of course, if you're really curious . . .

Polishing, dusting, and sweeping all lend themselves to the same imaginative self-deception. What does it actually matter whether you follow a cloth, a broom, or a vacuum? In the end, something else will hold sway for a while and get you to the other side at the same time. As you contemplate the handiwork of your cloth, broom, or vacuum, you can ask yourself truthfully whether you could have done any better. If the answer is "Yes," and you feel urgent about it, by all means go back and repair the handiwork, either without any more nonsense or with a few movement flourishes thrown in. If the answer is "No," put your vacuum (or cloth, or broom) away with special grace.

Chapter 6

TURNING TIME ON YOUR HANDS INTO MOVEMENT

Waiters aren't peculiar to restaurants. They're found all over. In fact there's no place on earth where someone isn't waiting for the doctor, the mailman, the elevator, the teller at the bank, the light to change, the sun to shine, the plane to take off, the plane to land, the children to return, the car to be fixed, the rain to stop. The list is endless.

In all this waiting, you're tilted ahead of yourself; you're future-oriented. But how about the present moment, right now? How about the actual situation in which you find yourself? While you might have the possibility of a magazine, a conversation, or the passing scene to distract you while you wait, you also have the possibility of yea-saying your own aliveness by putting movement into your life. Waiting is a goldmine of opportunities for doing two things at once.

Standing-Waiting Doodles

Suppose you're in a line at the post office, the supermarket, or ticket counter. There's no better time to draw on the floor. Don't worry.

You don't need to get down on your hands and knees and whip out a crayon or piece of chalk to do this. What you do is doodle with your feet.

You already know how to doodle with your toes. Doodling with your feet is obviously similar, but it's also very different, particularly when you're waiting in line. Here, at least one of your feet is supporting you at all times—you can't doodle with both feet at once as you might while you're sitting and talking on the phone—and you can't easily unwrap your feet and let them loose on their own.

There are further differences. Doodling with your feet while standing in line is less delicate than toe-dance doodling. For one thing, the lines aren't as fine as in toe-dancing. And foot-doodling usually doesn't involve dabs and pecks—though it certainly could, and in fact, heels as well as toes could dab and peck. But normally, foot doodling consists simply in drawing continuous, non-stop-till-you're-finished-with-whatever-you're-drawing lines.

You can draw all kinds of shapes from circles to figure eights to spirals to triangles to trapezoids. You can draw figures no one has ever heard of or named. You might be surprised at how much better one foot is than the other. Its movement feels more fluid. With a little pulse-taking and practice, you're sure to improve on your less-favored foot—to the point you become an ambidextrous foot-doodler.

Similar doodles are at your fingertips. When you're waiting in line your arms often hang down at your side. If you're empty-handed, why not trace out some forms, including all those no-name but perfectly reputable linear patterns with your fingertips? You can doodle with all eight fingers simultaneously if you're doubly empty, or you can doodle with one finger at a time. For a real challenge, try figure eights in opposite directions, the finger or fingers of one hand going one way, the finger or fingers of the other going the other way. Since there's no limit on lines—including the one you're waiting in—you can amuse yourself with possibilities for as long as you like. You can even try moving your hand and foot together in a duet.

Waiting-in-line doodles can be small or large. Whatever you feel comfortable with. The larger the pattern, the more your whole leg and arm are involved. If you prefer more modest doodles-while-you-wait, remember you can always indulge yourself more voluminously when you're waiting at home.

But suppose now you're standing on the street waiting for the bus or for some friends to arrive. Since you don't have to hold your place in a line, you can move around and surprise yourself with some sidewalk doodling. You can go literally in circles, for example. Or you can take a walk in spirals, domes, rhomboids, or rectangles. You can create more intricate and elaborate patterns by walking out letters on the sidewalk . . . or writing your name . . . or writing the number of the bus you're waiting for. The possibilities are quite open. Whatever stirs your imagination and moves you to move will steer you in the right direction.

Actually, whatever you can do with a pencil you can do with your body or parts of your body. This isn't so strange when you stop to think about it. When you doodle or write with a pencil, you're making circles and squiggles and strokes in your hand movements just as you're making circles, squiggles, and strokes on the piece of paper. You don't usually notice your hand movements because they're so very small and so habitual. But if you take time to notice yourself in the act of pencil doodling or writing, you'll surprise yourself. You can see all the different letter shapes in your movement. You can't only see them, you can feel them.

You can feel them even better if you close your eyes.

You can feel them still better if you keep your eyes closed and let go of your pencil but keep on writing.

Try some fake writing at the bus stop. When you do, you'll come to appreciate that your pencil is simply doing what your movement is doing: making lines—curved, straight, jagged, smooth lines (a fact that incidentally explains why your handwriting has the particular and unique graphic character it has). If you want to smooth out your writing, for example, or change it in any way, write some airy letters to your friends while you're waiting for the bus—in the handwriting of your choice, of course.

One last thought on doodling. As indicated above, whatever you can do with a pencil, you can do with parts of your body, many different parts of your body—not just hands and feet. Elbows can doodle, for example, knees can doodle, heads and hips can doodle. Each has its own idiosyncratic way of doodling. But even with such individuality, and regardless of its place or position in life, everything that doodles writes the same language—which is why, all by yourself, you can have a doodling party, or even a competition, while you wait. All of you can be invited and take part.

Standing–Waiting Slouches

Alas! By now your friends or the bus could have come and gone. If you're still waiting though, you might like to try a few slouches: round-trip sideward slouches.

Good round-trip sideward slouches are made up of well-synchronized knee and hip movements—opposite knee and hip movements.

You know how you stand sometimes when you're waiting with your weight on one leg—the hip on that standing leg jutting out to the side, and the knee of the opposite leg deeply flexed? You're standing in a sideward slouch. All of your weight is on one leg; the foot of your free leg is on the ground slightly forward of your standing leg.

Let's say you're sideward slouching to the right. Your left leg is relatively free. Your left foot is resting on the sidewalk. Let it rest just to the side instead of side and forward. What you're going to do is change your sideward slouch from right to left, something you've undoubtedly done many times before, but not in a slow, smooth, and deliberate way as now. You're going to notice yourself in transit and feel the stuff of which A-1 sideward slouches are made.

First let yourself gradually come up as far on the right side as you can. In other words, slowly unslouch yourself upward at the same time that you gradually move your right hip back to center and extend your left knee. As you do this, you'll find your left foot beginning to assume some weight. Let your weight keep shifting to the left till your left foot has it all and your left knee comes gradually to a full extension. Then let your left hip keep moving left, passing outside of center and all the way out to the left side. As you're doing this, let your right knee gradually flex, and continue flexing as far as it will go while still keeping your foot on the ground. The more you flex, the more you'll find yourself sinking down into your sideward slouch to the left, as if you were sinking into the billowy cushions of a plushy wall instead of a couch.

Waiting was never so comfortable. Each side of you gets a rest. When you come up high on one side and keep that high as your hips are in transit, you're guaranteed a good long descent. You can settle in for as long as you like before making the return trip.

Sitting–Waiting

What is it like when you're sitting someplace and waiting? In an office, a car, the dentist's chair, or at the laundromat?

You cross your arms at the wrist and rest your hands on your lap. Then you uncross them and rest your hands on your thighs. Or you cross your arms by folding one inside the other, then uncross them and rest your chin on one hand. Very often you cross and uncross your legs. Just as often, you cross and uncross your feet.

However you embellish sitting and waiting with crossings and uncrossings, you don't really think about what's moving—or what's moveable. You think about sitting and waiting—and about how much longer it's going to be.

When you're sitting and waiting, what is moveable? Legs, arms, faces, rib cages, shoulders, spines. Actually, a lot more than you might at first think.

Suppose you're waiting in a doctor's office. People read magazines, talk quietly, or stare vacantly ahead. There's sometimes a nervous calm to the atmosphere as if everyone were sitting on eggs, not to hatch them but because brooding on something comes with the office. You sense a hushed quietness mixed with everything from impatience to anxiety, boredom to resentment at having to wait so long. In short, the place could definitely stand an infusion of positive, life-proclaiming spirit.

Putting movement into your waiting-for-the-doctor life can be as refreshing as putting movement into your cleaning life. To find that refreshment you have only to lift a finger and more.

You don't usually do anything at the doctor's unless asked: "Lie down on the table," "Take this bottle and . . . ." In general, you feel yourself to be in someone else's hands. Maybe that's why the office calm is nervous and the reverence mixed. Yet what better place to proclaim your aliveness? What better place to feel your aliveness and let it regenerate you to the point that it sees you through whatever miseries have brought you here in the first place?

The first yea-saying thing to do is to raise your arms overhead, slowly and evenly, and feel your lungs begin naturally to fill up with air as your hands just clear your head and ascend to their full reach. When you feel your lungs begin to fill up in this way, let your head tilt backward, slowly and evenly, until your chin is as up as it was in Chapter 5. Pause here for a moment. Then let your arms begin a slow and even descent by flexing at the elbows. As your hands approach the sides of your head on their way down, let your head untilt, slowly and evenly, in concert with them.

You'll find yourself breathing out as your arms come down, if not from the start of their descent, then at least as your hands pass on either side of your head.

You might think it takes courage to do this movement amidst all these people. But stop and think: you tie your shoelaces in front of other people; you put on your coat in front of other people; you open the door in front of other people; you reach for the jam in front of other people. What you do in front of other people is move with objects, or in order to get hold of objects. But there's no law that says you can move in front of other people only if 1) you already have an object or 2) you're in pursuit of one. There's no law that says you can't move yourself as well as objects about. And there's no reason you have to wait till the doctor asks, "Can you still raise your arms overhead?" to move your arms overhead, as if such a movement were perverse apart from an object.

There's more to the courage story. When you see all these people waiting with you, remember you all have one thing in common—besides the fact that you're all waiting. You all have miseries of one kind or another. You and everyone else can wait and think that only someone else's hands can cure the misery, or you can wait and let your own hands—and more—ease your woes for a time. You can let the misery take you down and keep you down, or you can let your aliveness take you up—part of you literally up—and find a good breath of fresh air in the process.

Feelings of aliveness aren't pharmaceutically packageable. A breath of fresh air doesn't come in capsule form. The wonderful thing about movement is that besides being revitalizing, it's free and you don't have to wash it down with water. *(Ponderabilia 11: Synergies of Meaningful Movement)*

If you want to ease yourself discreetly into raising your arms overhead, use a normal everyday overhead stretch as a prelude. It gives the impression of being purposeful if not irrepressible. An overhead stretch is faster and more energetic than the arm-raising described above. It has a different dynamic quality. You can begin with an everyday stretch, then retrace your path in the manner described—as if you were studying in detail what you just did.

One final aspect to consider. The space into which your arms are reaching is vacant, absolutely clear of any objects. It's a completely open, bare, uninhabited space. When you raise your arms overhead, or stretch naturally, it's not as if you're disturbing someone by waving your arms in front of the magazine they're reading. You're not encroaching on their space in any way. What you're doing is feeling your way into what is, for all practical purposes, outer space—an area where no one lives and no one's likely to stake out a claim. Be adventurous!

But suppose now you're in a less open waiting-sitting situation: in a car while your friend's gone into the store.

Why not start out with some simple shoulder movements, first one shoulder, then the other: up and down, up and down; forward and back-to-center, forward and back-to-center? Take time to savor the movement. Do it slowly and gently several times over. Then move one shoulder really back, not just back to center, but back of center. Center is where you are when you're not forward or backward. It's where your shoulders are naturally before you move them. Move first one then the other shoulder back and center for a little while. A single warning: shoulders don't normally move backward as far as they can move forward, so don't let a passion for equal mobility trick you into straining for more when there is no more.

Now move your shoulders together, forward and back to center a few times, sensing a bit of an upward lift and then a release as you do so. You can feel a rhythm, a nice, even, easy rhythm when you do this. Let your toes enter into the rhythm—to whatever degree your shoes allow. (Actually, you might consider removing your shoes and allowing a little air to circulate.) Curl your toes up when your shoulders come forward and a bit upward and uncurl them when your shoulders go back down and to center.

There's a clear feeling that shoulders and toes are connected to each other: they come toward each other and then move away from each other. It's a pleasing and unusual relationship. If you didn't actually feel it in the flesh, you might never guess there could be such compatibility.

Moving is full of such discoveries. You just have to give things a little whirl of sorts to get started—in this instance, a little lift forward and an upward curl.

If car-sitting is more restricted than doctor's-office-sitting, then dentist-chair-sitting puts the ultimate squeeze on you.

What can you do in a dentist's chair while you're waiting for the X-rays to be developed, the anaesthetic to work, or the dentist to come back?

You can make faces. Faces beyond the one you may already be making as you're sitting there on the half-slant.

To begin with, you're not just there on the half-slant but in a virtually closed three-sided box. Something is peering down at you from above. What's more, you're surrounded: there's equipment to the right of you, equipment to the left of you, equipment in front of you, all of it seeming ready to discharge some electrical effect upon your personage. Moreover with all this equipment about, you don't have much elbow room.

In spite of everything, however, the situation is not entirely hopeless. Even if your mouth is open and some gadget is draped on it or is actually in it, you can still move your eyes, nose, and forehead; you can wink, blink, and maybe nod just a wee bit; you can raise your eyebrows as in surprise, lower them as in a frown, open your eyes wide, close them tightly, wrinkle your nose, roll your eyes, and wiggle your ears or scalp if your talents allow.

If your mouth isn't draped with some contraption or other—and/or if it isn't the temporary repository of some exotic material or prop—you can also move your mouth: you can smile; you can open up in a gargantuan yawn; you can move your jaw from side to side or jut it forward and put your bottom teeth on top of your top ones; you can stick out your tongue, wag it, and put it back in. In short, your movement possibilities are quite extraordinary considering the circumstances.

If you get more than one thing moving at a time, you can even orchestrate some avant-garde ensemble playing: you can wink and lift your eyebrows at the same time; you can wrinkle your nose and roll your eyes at the same time. Ask yourself what these expressions feel like, and what someone would think if you did them in public.

When you wink and lift your eyebrows, for example, are you about to sneeze? Or are you looking disdainfully at something beneath you?

When you wrinkle your nose and roll your eyes, are you signaling what the next play should be or are you commenting on the unfortunate one that was just made?

You certainly can't fall asleep while you're busy orchestrating or analyzing the possible meanings of your orchestrations. On the contrary, you'll be amazed—open-mouthed, so to speak—at how mobile your face is and how positively regenerating the making of faces can be. You'll feel stresses recede as you give yourself a facial of sorts, a lively "Look, Ma! No hands!" self-administered massage.

Actually the faces you move in and out of are no funnier than all of the equipment surrounding you. When you think that all this heavy stuff is designed for the small delicate opening that is your mouth, and that all those gadgets and dainty tools you see lying about are in fact going to enter into that opening and set up shop, well—there's something ludicrous about the disproportionate and incongruous parties involved as well as in the fact that they're actually going to meet in some highly intimate ways.

Just Plain Waiting

Have you ever been stuck in an airport terminal? You have a one-hour, three-hour, or even ten-hour wait. What on earth do you do in this closed, airless space in which you're a virtual captive?

You sit—most of the time you sit. *(Ponderabilia 12: On the Temporality of Our Aliveness)*

A wonderful way of revitalizing your sagging spirits and infusing yourself with some fresh if already used and bone-dry air is by some long-stride walking—the longest-stride walking of which you're capable. If you're daring, you can pretend every moment is so precious you must run. Never mind that you're longest-stride walking—or running—to an empty check-in counter. What does it matter if the counter's unmanned and absolutely no one is at the gate when you arrive? You can longest-stride walk to another counter to see if anything's going on there.

98

A good way to begin your walk is to reconnoiter the general environs first. This way you find out something of the layout of the place you're going to before you start. You don't have to avoid busy areas when you're striding forth. But remember too that longest-stride walking doesn't have to be at the speed of light. You can walk at whatever pace you feel comfortable with.

When you enliven yourself and your circulation by making strides at any speed, your legs particularly will appreciate the change. Your lower legs will feel lighter than they could possibly feel, hanging hour after hour from your knees with nothing to do. And your thighs, which are otherwise lying lifeless as day-old pancakes on the seat of the chair, will get a resounding new lease on life too.

When you go longest-stride walking, don't forget to take your arms along with you. When they do some longest-stride swinging in concert with your legs, you'll get an even greater boost of spirit.

Now suppose you've finally made your connection and have arrived home. You'd like a cup of freshly brewed tea or coffee and are waiting for the water to boil. You have a little time on your hands. Why not try a one-leg horizontal stand while you're waiting?

First, find something stable like the edge of a table that you can hold onto at arms' length. Be sure it has a fair amount of free space in front of it. A floor model TV will do as nicely as a table. So will a sink counter if there's the requisite amount of room. By the way, arms' distance means both arms: you're facing whatever you're holding onto, not standing sideways to it. And you don't actually have to hold onto the table. It's fine simply to rest your fingers or hands on its top surface.

Next, make sure your feet are a bit more than arms' length away from whatever edge you're attached to. Make sure by feeling as well as seeing where you are. If your feet are more than arms' length away from the edge, then your shoulders will be closest to the edge, your hips further away, and your feet the furthest away. In other words, you'll be tilted forward just slightly.

Now slowly begin lifting your right leg in back of you. At about the point when your toes clear the floor, your torso will want to come downward, that is, tilt forward from the hip joint, your left hip joint. Your elbows will naturally begin bending as well.

Keep raising your leg and lowering your torso until torso and leg are on a horizontal line. If your leg doesn't want to go up that high, don't force it. A one-leg diagonal stand is fine too. Whether you end at the diagonal or at the horizontal, if your leg and torso are moving smoothly together, they'll be in the kind of relationship that seesaw boards are in: as one goes up, the other goes down; when neither is going up or down, they're perfectly balanced—as in a horizontal line.

The reciprocal movements are there by courtesy of the hip joint of your standing leg. The joint is as fine a fulcrum as any seesaw wedge and allows the same easy, fluid ride up and down.

Where's your head in all this activity? Certainly it's following along, but the flow of movement is at its simplest best if your head stays docilely in the same bodily relationship it was in before you started moving: if your head stays perched on top of your torso as at the beginning and doesn't tilt backward, you'll end up looking straight down at the floor. On the way you'll have seen whatever sights come into view. The general feeling will be of a passing scene going by.

One-leg diagonal or horizontal lines are a pleasant diversion when you're caught betwixt and between in waiting situations. They bring up what was down and bring down what was up and give you a new point of view on the world in the process.

But suppose now you have a longer wait. Perhaps you're standing at the washing machine waiting for it to fill, or for the dryer to complete its cycle so you can whisk out the clothes and be on your way. You can surprise yourself while you wait by shifting your attention and shifting something else besides: your weight, from both legs to just one.

When your weight is fully and comfortably on one leg and the other foot is resting weightless on the floor, lift that weightless foot and begin moving the leg backward as if you were taking a preparatory backswing prior to kicking something in front of you. Then let it simply drop-swing forward and then backward, forward and backward, in nice, easy drop-swings.

You can feel the drop-swing best if your swinging knee remains slightly flexed. Your foot then sweeps across the floor smoothly on its way forward and back. Your swinging leg movement doesn't need to be large, but it should be from the hip joint so that the movement is of the whole leg and not just from the knee down. If you swing your leg only from the knee down, then your swinging knee will pass your standing knee in a forward direction only. To find the most enjoyable swing quality possible, let your swinging knee pass your standing knee coming and going.

If you want to, you can turn sideways to the machine and give yourself some reassuring but light support by resting your hand on it as you swing your outside leg—the leg on the opposite side of your hand.

You can hum a little tune while you're swinging.

After a while, shift your weight to the free-swinging leg and drop-swing your other leg. If you're swinging with some light support, turn around and let your other hand rest on the machine. Feel the looseness of your swinging leg as it goes by, forward and backward.

And keep humming.

If the water is still coming in or the clothes still aren't dry, try a variation:

Facing the machine, shift your weight again fully to one leg—say the left one. Bring your right knee upward, not directly in front of your chest but far enough toward your right shoulder so that you don't bang your knee on the machine. Now lower your right leg, shift your weight onto it, and raise your left knee. Alternate this lifting and lowering of legs. What you've got is a slightly outward-to-the-side and exaggerated in-place march or tramp, as in "Tramp, tramp, tramp, the boys are marching!"

Sometimes it's startling to hear joints creak. Don't be alarmed. Change your tune and sing a slow march to drown out the noise.

If you're still waiting for the water to reach its peak or for the clothes to dry, try something a bit more complicated.

Shift your weight to one leg and raise your other knee upward and slightly to the side as before, but instead of then lowering that leg and shifting your weight to it, extend the foreleg as if you were about to reach out and scoop something in with it. Now, without separating the reaching movement from the scooping movement, do scoop your leg back toward you, pulling it back as you lower it. When your foot approximates the floor, let it slide along the floor toward your standing leg.

The movement doesn't actually describe a circle, but it has a circular feel to it: you raise your knee to the side, reach out with your foreleg, scoop your foreleg back toward you as you lower it, then slide your foot on the floor till your scooping leg meets your standing leg. It's as if your raised, reaching, and scooping leg is bicycling its way to the side all by itself.

If balance is a problem, remember what you learned in Chapter 3: a minimum of effort and a maximum of effect.

Remember too: you're not trying to impress the neighbors—or yourself. Small circular feelings are as good as large ones.

Feeling alive comes in all sizes.

Chapter 7

THE JOYS OF MOVING NOW AND THEN OR KNOWING THE SOURCE OF YOUR ALIVENESS FROM THE INSIDE OUT

Moving now and then means living beyond fitness of any kind. When you put movement into your life, you're not thinking about physical conditioning, bigger muscles, thinner thighs, or what have you. You're putting movement into your life to awaken yourself to the life you're living. When you move not for your body—for its good—but for yourself, when you begin giving yourself a breath of fresh air and listening to yourself breathe, you find being alive is a splendid way of being all by itself. A sense of aliveness elongates along the lines of your body, dissipating stressful tensions and restoring a zestful vitality.

How do you start putting movement into your life? You start whenever you want and with whatever strikes your fancy. There are no rules and no set procedures. And there are no special clothes you have to wear. Whatever you're wearing at the moment is exactly what you need to wear. You'll probably find that loose-fitting clothes allow you to move more freely and spontaneously, that the flow and range of your movement is unimpeded by counter-pulls. When it comes to shoes and socks, the more often you can dispense with them—and feel comfortable dispensing with them—the better. But the rule here too is that there is no rule. Putting movement into your life is not any kind of special dress occasion. It's an occasion simply for waking up to the joys of moving, and whatever you happen to be wearing when you wake up is what you've decided to wear—or not wear.

You don't have to go any place special either to savor the joys of moving now and then. You're wherever you happen to be when you start living beyond fitness—in the bathtub, at the post office, in the car or kitchen, at the bus stop or bank. It's not the place that makes the difference: you make the difference. You can wake up to the joys of movement virtually anywhere and have a nice time.

There are more non-rules.

Not only don't you need to follow a set procedure, change clothes, or drive off to a special place, you don't need to warm up. You're already warmed up because you're already alive. Granted this aliveness is commonly, even routinely, in the background. It can be brought to the foreground instantaneously: a turn, a tilt, a circle, a lift, a simple movement here and there, and Presto! You're putting movement into your life with whatever bodily inclinations come your way.

In living beyond fitness, you're not either bent on doing something with your body. You're not running it through any regimen or through any paces. And you're not trying to make it perform this or that feat either. You're simply initiating a process, and letting the process happen to you in the sense that you're listening to it. You're not pushing it along, prodding it this way and that, or trying to impress anyone. You're not standing over it with any kind of ruler. You're simply moving and listening to yourself moving.

When you realize your aliveness in this way, you realize there are no right and wrong ways of doing any of the movements described here—short of doing them in ways you find easy and natural and not in ways you're not enjoying. You realize that whatever the movement sequence, you start out easily and with small rather than large intentions. Actually, you're not likely to end up pushing yourself around at all when you go with the idea of natural and fluid movement. You don't strain yourself. You know you can always move more fully the next time around if you choose. You know you can always increase the speed after you've gotten the feel of the movement.

There's a built-in benefit in this realization. When you start relatively small and at a leisurely pace, you're more likely to be in touch with your body all the way along and to appreciate its—or rather, your—limits. You're more likely to be in touch with yourself and aware of the tension you're starting out with and how to release it if there's a surplus. In other words, you're more likely to be listening to your kinesthetic self, to be putting an ear to your movement and sensing its qualitative dynamics.

The more you become used to moving and listening in this way—to feeling yourself feeling your way along—the more attuned you become to your weaknesses and strengths, your limitations and powers of movement. And the more you come to know the integrity of your own body, when enough is enough, and when more is refreshing. *(Ponderabilia 13: Thinking in Movement)*

When you divide your life into movement times and other-than-movement times, you package your life in ways that may be effective in terms of working and playing, socializing and being alone, taking care of practicalities and sitting back and being entertained. But when it comes to movement, the division is not wholly effective; you're not getting the maximum of movement benefits. For one thing, what you're doing in the way of scheduled movement—whether it's exercising, jogging, swimming, aerobics, or whatever—it cannot be re-done during the day to make a difference when you need a little change, a little refreshment, a little relaxation from stresses and strains. Certainly there's a spillover from these activities—a decidedly enlivening one. It would be surprising if there weren't. You feel energized. Your spirits are renewed. But you can't tap into that vitality at later points of the day when you feel the need of a lift, unless of course you go for another jog, to another exercise class, or for another swim or round of aerobics.

When you make an East-is-East-and-West-is-West-and-never-the-twain-shall-meet division between movement and non-movement times, you're certain to wake up to the joys of movement for certain periods during the day, but you don't know these joys intimately as part of your everyday, ongoing being. They're not at your fingertips. Perhaps you don't even realize that they could be there at all. In effect, you miss the possibility of drawing on an enormous reserve of potential energy and spirit. Knowing the source of your aliveness from the inside out is being able to vitalize and celebrate your aliveness on a moment's notice.

Of course you can have the best of all possible worlds and move in both scheduled and unscheduled ways. The one doesn't exclude the other. And it's certainly not a matter of choosing either one or the other. It's nice to have a wallop of a shot of movement as in jogging or swimming. A wallop of movement is, well, a wallop of movement, a wonderful huffy-puffy, stir-up-the-juices exhilaration that can reverberate energy for hours. But a wallop doesn't automatically or necessarily spread itself out over the whole day. No matter how moving the experience, once you've had it, you've had it. It's indeed nice to sprinkle a bit of less structured, easy-going, explorative and creative movement here and there throughout the day, interweaving it with the rest of your everyday concerns and affairs, and even with those wallops. Moving now and then is rejuvenating in the way that time-release capsules are rejuvenating: a little bit through the whole day keeps things perking.

Moving now and then means enjoying movement for its own sake. In this respect it's childlike and non-mechanical. There's a connection between the two characteristics.

To begin with, how you feel your aliveness depends on how you move, and how you move depends in good measure on how you once learned to move yourself about. Learning to move yourself about was something you did as a child, not only walking, but reaching, pushing, pulling, banging, hopping, skipping, and so on. There was a delight in this moving and a sense of discovery. If there weren't, you'd never have taken your first step.

When this zest for movement dies, something of your aliveness dies with it. A peculiar mobility takes over. This is because you no longer feel any moving center: little or no breath of life survives in your torso—in your chest, pelvis, back, or abdomen. Lacking little or no breath, your torso may indeed be a storehouse of immobilizing tensions. Aliveness is in turn reduced to survival-moving hands and feet, peripheral gestures at the end of your being. Survival-moving hands and feet move in restricted, repetitive, predictable patterns. New dimensions rarely open up.

Robots move in this way. They have hands and feet, but their torsos aren't primed with life at all. In fact, they have no real torso, only a box-like centerpiece that doesn't move. It's not supple in the least degree. Most important, a robot is wired neither for moving itself on its own inclinations nor for feeling the dynamics of its own movement. A dimension of being is clearly missing. Certainly there's circuitry that serves to connect the limbs to a central body, but the central body is kinesthetically and kinetically deaf and dumb.

You can see box-like centerpieces almost any day on any street, in any bank or supermarket. They're recognizable by their stiff, unbending shapes. But box-like centerpieces like these can transform themselves— into their original vibrant, movement-sensitive, movement-delighting selves. How? By rediscovering their aliveness from the inside out. So transformed, they're not childish but childlike in that the gift of movement is celebrated and its enjoyment knows no bounds.

Savoring the joys of movement is really an ageless way of yea-saying your aliveness.

When the joys of movement are bottled up, they get wrinkled. When you release them from captivity, they take wing. They have air to breathe again. *(Ponderabilia VI: On Unsteady Souls, the Fleetingness of Movement, and the Imaginative Consciousness of Movement)*

We can dig up an old word to remind ourselves that, whatever our age, we're in fact movable, moving creatures, and that even as we might lose some of our suppleness and strength as we get older, we're still alive and well and living someplace in the world. We're still, as D. H. Lawrence once said, "alive and in the flesh and part of the living incarnate cosmos." The word *coenesthesis* means a sensing of the whole body—a sense of full-bodied aliveness. There are no special sense organs for this whole-body sensing, but it's clearly generated by the body, and it comes most keenly and vividly to the fore in moving. If we're going to dig that word up and use it again, we'd better justify its resurrection and show how very real and meaningful a sense it has.

Coenesthesis disappeared from usage some years ago, probably because a sense of aliveness came to be regarded as a hokum sense; it was without proper papers. By Western scientific standards, any sense worth its salt has a sense organ attached to it; no sense organ, no sense. But "sense of aliveness" is not just a figure of speech. It's something very real to us, something we even cherish. The puzzle disappears the moment we realize that we're not only specimens for scientific investigation and analysis; we're also alive, in the first-person sense of aliveness. We don't have to submit to a test or ask around for validation or confirmation of this fact.

Clearly, there's more to the reality of being alive than meets the scientific eye. It's called coenesthesis, a sense called forth most dramatically and vitally by self-movement. To get in touch with your coenesthetic self, you don't retire to the nearest easy chair and wait for a sense of aliveness to wash over you. Kinesthesis and coenesthesis are related, as related as they look and sound. Let's start at the beginning and spell out their connection.

Kinesthetic awarenesses are the most fundamental awarenesses any creature could possibly have—more fundamental than vision. You can't unfeel yourself in the same way you can close your eyes, and even when you close your eyes, you still feel yourself. Most important, when it comes to movement, kinesthetic awarenesses are different from visual ones.

Suppose you're in a movement class of some kind. What do you do?

You observe what someone's doing, then try your hand at it. In the best of circumstances, you're encouraged to pay attention to the dynamics you're creating—to the feel of your movement as you're moving. You're encouraged, in other words, to listen to what you're feeling kinesthetically and not just replicate the movement you see before you.

In less than optimum circumstances, you get less than optimum benefits. You're so busy trying to emulate the moving body you see in front of you that you're short-changing the body you are, and are thus short-changing the experience of living in your own movement. What you ultimately short-change is the possibility of playing with the movement sequences you're in the process of learning. When you don't make the movement your own by listening to it and letting it captivate you with its dynamics, routines of movement become routine in every sense.

When you live in the visual reality of movement, you might be concerned with your ability—or inability—to turn your leg this way or that. You might be concerned with your ability to replicate to the letter all of the movements of your instructor or to do a movement as well as your neighbor. If your attention is consistently fixed on such matters, however, then your bodily awarenesses are overwhelmingly in the service of the visual, and the experience of living in your own movement is cut short.

When you're living in your own movement, your concern with the visual is only as a blueprint for moving autonomously. The center of your concern is with how the movement feels, not with what it—or you—looks like. You feel whatever dynamic happenings are happening—the particular flow of energy that makes this particular movement what it is and not some other movement. You feel the richness and all the subtleties of form that enter into this unique dynamic. But that's not all you feel. When you tune in on kinesthetic happenings, you're on the brink of discovering coenesthetic ones.

Coenesthesis comes in because you're making differences as well as noticing them; that is, you're making things happen! We haven't talked about making differences in quite this way before, but the connection has been there all along and is immediately obvious. Making differences doesn't only mean becoming aware of your movement habits—your same old movement prints—and in turn changing them, infusing them with new life. It means becoming aware of your own creative movement possibilities, your power to invent, improvise, shape, and rework any movement. When you give yourself free reign, you discover that making differences comes naturally. You discover in turn that your potential for movement is as much a matter of your potential for making differences as your capacity for making differences is a matter of your capacity for movement.

A bit dense or doubtful? Not at all. In making differences, it's you who are creating the changing shapes and spaces, the changing rhythms and flows of energy, the changing kinesthetically felt dynamics. No one else is making these kinetic happenings happen. They're your creation. It's not the fact, then, but the feeling of creation that's connected with coenesthesis. In moving creatively and making differences, you discover precisely your power to make things happen. You feel the fun and vitality of creation. A sensing of your whole body—a sense of full-bodied aliveness—rides high on these feelings of fun and vitality. It's very much an exhilarating, full-bodied feeling. It's a yea-saying feeling. It's a celebration of livingness that reaches into, fills, and radiates out of every cranny of your being.

When you're in touch with your aliveness from the inside out, you're in touch with both kinesthetic and coenesthetic happenings. You're beyond conditioning, fitness, and exercising. You're at the pulsing center of your own splendid, ever-changing livingness.

Why not surprise yourself in an experience of that livingness right now?

And why not make a habit of surprising yourself now and then?

Why not explore the source of your aliveness from the inside out?

In other words, why not put movement into your life?

Ponderabilia 1:

ON MOVEMENT AND FEELING ALIVE

If you were asked to describe the relationship of movement to feeling alive, you might simply say that when you're awake, you're moving about doing this and that and feel alive in the doing, and that when you lie down and go to sleep, you're actually still alive but don't feel it because you're asleep. Specifying when you can and can't feel your aliveness though is only a beginning answer. The deeper challenge is to describe your experience of the actual dynamics that constitute your feelings of aliveness.

Clearly there is a difference between the animate and the inanimate. When a body is inanimate, it might indeed be dead, for to be dead is precisely to be unmoving. There is no breath, no pulsing heartbeat, nary a twitter. There is nothing to feel for there is no feeling body. All is still—permanently.

D. H. Lawrence eloquently described the difference between the animate and the inanimate when he wrote, "Whatever the unborn and the dead may know, they cannot know the beauty, the marvel of being alive in the flesh. The dead may look after the afterwards. But the magnificent here and now of life in the flesh is ours, and ours alone, and ours only for a time. We ought to dance with rapture that we should be alive and in the flesh, and part of the living, incarnate cosmos" (Lawrence 1932, pp. 199-200).

When you put movement into your life, you may not be dancing with rapture or feel yourself part of the living incarnate cosmos, but you will certainly feel yourself alive and in the flesh. Why? Because putting movement into your life awakens your kinesthetically felt body, and in notably dynamic ways. When movement itself is the focal point of attention, kinetic dynamics come to the fore. The kinetic dynamics involve gradations in tension, shifts in direction, changes in amplitude and in the continuity of movement—all in the process of something as simple as scrubbing a pot. Kinetic dynamics structure our everyday doings. They are what dynamic systems scholar J. A. Scott Kelso—a Pierre Fermat laureate and founder and longtime director of the Center for Complex Systems and Brain Sciences at Florida Atlantic University—has studied and written about in his lifelong work on coordination dynamics, the dynamics of experienced movement patternings and correlated brain patternings that inform our everyday lives (Kelso 1995; Kelso and Engstrøm 2006; Jantzen, Steinberg, and Kelso 2008; Oullier and Kelso 2009). Coordination dynamics—dynamics that are kinetic through and through—are indeed at the core of our very being.

In spite of their elemental significance, kinetic dynamics informing everyday experience are typically submerged in the course of our daily doings. The dynamics are submerged because our kinesthetically felt body is submerged. The instrumental body—the one that's busy getting things done—dampens experience of that body. Not that kinesthetic dynamics are totally unfelt—it's not as if we were anesthetized—but that the movement dynamics of our everyday habits of moving about in the world tend to be in the background rather than the foreground of attention. Moreover kinesthetically felt dynamics may also be submerged because in this age of speeded-up doings, people are too busy getting things done to turn attention to their own movement. There's virtually no time for feeling alive.

Yet at one time in our lives, we all were all riveted on movement, our own movement and the movement of everything about us. With no prior tutoring whatsoever, we took what is living to be that which moves itself and to apprehend what is not moving and has never moved to be inanimate. Indeed, we intuitively grasped the coincidence of aliveness and animation from the very beginning.

More than thirty years ago—well before mirror neurons came into prominence and testified in neurological ways (at least in macaque monkeys) to the distinction between the animate and the inanimate—René Spitz, a well-known Swiss psychiatrist, honed in on the fact that what is animate does two things: it consistently captures the attention of infants and elicits a response. What reliably does both in infant life is the "percept of the human face and eyes" and the "perception of movement of any kind" (Spitz 1983, pp. 148-149). Daniel Stern's more recent studies deepen Spitz's basic observations by specifying animation in more exacting ways. Stern, an infant psychiatrist and clinical psychologist, describes the sensitivity of infants to "vitality affects," that is, how infants experience the purely "dynamic, kinetic" nature of a phenomenon, as in bursts of light or laughter, attenuated sounds or images, fleeting figures or aromas. He furthermore analyzes in detail how the intensity, timing, and shape of movement undergird the affective attunement evident between infant and parent, an attunement in which the quality of feeling of an infant's movement is dynamically reflected in the parent's response (Stern 1985).

In a sense, this book leads you back to infancy, recapturing that time before language when you were attentive and alive not just to the kinetic dynamics about you, but to your own kinesthetic dynamics, your own movement, exploring its possibilities in creative ways, indeed, exploring its vitality affects and attunements. Putting movement into your life doesn't ask you to pretend to be an infant again, trying to hoist yourself up along the edge of a coffee table, for example. It asks you simply to attend to your own moving body, which is precisely what we all once did as infants. Indeed, we all had to learn our bodies and learn to move ourselves—and without an owner's manual! And without instructions from anyone! We made inchoate reaching movements, we kicked our legs, we grasped things, we opened and closed our fingers, we made and unmade a fist, we turned ourselves over, we turned things over in our hands, we threw things, and so on. We were enjoying our own primal animation. We discovered movement possibilities and developed our native kinetic talents, forging them ultimately into a repertoire of everyday patterns of movement (Sheets-Johnstone 1999/ expanded 2nd ed. 2011). We forged a relatively vast and varied range of "I cans" on the foundation of "I move."

In the course of growing up, we typically learn to regulate our natural kinetic surges and creative dispositions, that is, our natural kinesthetically felt inclinations, in accordance with familial, social, and educational constraints. In turn, our exploration of movement and of our movement possibilities comes to a relative standstill; our kinetic imagination falls dormant. We may find all kinds of wonderful,

118

satisfying sport activities to be engaged in, but we no longer engage in and treasure movement for its own sake. Our original connection of movement with animation and with feelings of aliveness is broken.

When we engage in creative movement enterprises again, we regenerate the connection, and the feeling of aliveness blossoms once again. The feeling is not a lasting one but follows the course of our movement itself. Dancer/choreographer Merce Cunningham gives us a keen sense of the connection and the feeling when he comments that "you have to love dancing to stick to it. it gives you nothing back, no manuscripts to store away, no paintings to show on walls and maybe hang in museums, no poems to be printed and sold, nothing but that single fleeting moment when you feel alive. it is not for unsteady souls" (Cunningham 1968, unpaginated).

There'll be time later to ponder "unsteady souls" and more later too on the fleeting character of movement. For now, a few parting words about moving in an everyday sense in light of Cunningham's remark about dancing—about loving it and about what it gives back to you.

When you put movement into your life, no one is taking pictures for posterity or notating your movement; no one is complimenting you on your agility or giving accolades for your creativity; no one is there waiting to interview you; and so on. You're not moving as in a dance concert. You're moving for yourself alone, for the sheer experience of your own movement. In both fleeting instances, however, because it is a question of movement, you're open to the experience of feeling alive. In both fleeting instances, "you have to love" what you're doing not just to stick with it, but to have the kinesthetically felt experience of movement in the first place, and to cherish its dynamic if fleeting reality.

A sum-up ponder thought: Aliveness is a concept grounded in animation. The concept comes to life—you feel alive—when you move for the sake of movement itself.

Ponderabilia 2:

IT'S AMAZING!

It's amazing that in this 21st century we are still under the illusion that we have only five senses!

Conventional wisdom tells us that vision, hearing, touch, smell, and taste constitute the sum total. It is true enough that these senses are our sensory windows on the world, but it is certainly not true that they are the sum total of our senses or we could hardly get about efficiently in the world: we would be oblivious of our own movement! We could hardly reach and grasp or put one foot ahead of the next and transfer weight effectively.

The sequence of development of embryonic neural tissue implicitly underscores the significance of proprioception and kinesthesia and thereby the significance of self-movement. Beginning development of the semicircular ear canals which, through vestibular sensations, provide a sense of balance or imbalance takes place in the fourth week of intrauterine life. Beginning development of muscles which, through kinesthesia, provide a sense of movement and position takes place before the eleventh week, making lip opening and closing, for example, forehead wrinkling, and head turning possible.

The comparatively early development of neural tissue related to movement is of particular interest in conjunction with physiological studies suggesting that neural development of the motor cortex is stimulated by the body movements of the fetus itself. In other words, form does not develop solely on its own. Movement influences morphology. Myelination studies also show that motor neurons myelinate early and that acoustic-vestibular neurons myelinate next. In short, however unacknowledged and indeed insufficiently valued in studies of developmental neurology, kinesthesia and proprioception are of central import to our lives as animate beings. (For readings on embryonic and fetal development, see Furuhjelm, Ingelman-Sundbert, and Wirsén 1976; Robeck 1978; Windle 1971.)

It is furthermore amazing in light of the ongoing sophisticated age of science in which we live—specifically, the domains of neuroscience and cognitive science, and their offshoots in a variety of disciplines—that kinesthesia continues to go unrecognized and certainly insufficiently valued. When we hear and read about motor control, motor learning, motor skills, and so on, we are actually hearing and reading about something distant from experience. Indeed, we don't experience nerve firings any more than we experience our brains! Notable neuroscientists nevertheless tell us of just such experiences. For example, Francis Crick and Christof Koch write, "If you see the back of a person's head, the brain infers that there is a face on the front of it" (Crick and Koch 1992, p. 153); Semir Zeki writes, "An object's image varies with distance, yet the brain can ascertain its true size" (Zeki 1992, p. 69). Moreover we find articles on such topics as "How the brain knows when eating must stop" (Raloff 1996, p. 341) and "The Brain as a Darwin Machine," in which we learn that a brain "shapes up thoughts in milliseconds rather than millennia, and uses innocuous remembered environments rather than the noxious real-life ones" (Calvin 1987, p. 33).

The examples could actually go on and on, and include not only experiential ascriptions to human brains as above, but general ascriptions that are also at times downright comical, as in the statement, "Nonhuman primates have brains capable of cooperative hunting" (Harding 1975, p. 255). It's as if nonhuman primate brains rolled forth together on the savannah in search of something to eat. In short, the brain that we continually hear and read about is conceived to be the oracle at Delphi, the place to which so many present-day scientists and others academics address the particular question that concerns them, the place to which they look for solutions to the particular problem that baffles them, including most notably the mind/body problem. When we follow along uncritically and unreflectively in deference to this 21st century oracle, we in truth divorce ourselves from the experience of our living bodies. We lose touch with our dynamically engaged kinesthetically-attuned selves, distancing ourselves from the very animation that drives and structures our lives.

Finally, it is amazing that in this pivotally focused age of "embodiment" in which virtually all human faculties are academically qualified—one might even say "anointed"—by being "embodied," as in "embodied mind," "embodied language," "embodied simulation," "embodied self-awareness," "embodied agency," "embodied experience," "embodied cognition," "embodied emotions" (e.g., Thompson 2007, Varela, Thompson, and Rosch 1991; Lakoff and Johnson 1999; Freedberg and Gallese 2007; Gallagher 2000; Gibbs 2006), and even— wonder of wonders!—"embodied movement" (Gibbs 2006, Varela and Depraz 2005)—kinesthesia is nowhere on the map.

In each instance, the qualifier "embodied" is pasted on whatever faculty is being considered and the faculty is thereby given a real place in the world. But the term 'embodiment' and its derivatives are in fact nothing more than a lexical band-aid covering over a still suppurating three-hundred-seventy-five-year-old wound: 17th French philosopher René Descartes's division of mind and body. In using the term, people are actually perpetuating a divide that has not healed and will never heal so long as they ignore the realities of our basic animation (Sheets-Johnstone 1999a, 1999b/2011). Animation is the key to resolving the underlying division that remains part of their thinking. Why? Because in reality, we do not experience ourselves or others as embodied—that is, packaged like cans of frozen orange juice! We experience ourselves first and foremost as alive, moving and being moved in and by the world around us, as when we are curious to explore a new idea or new vista, or when we turn a possible course of action over in our mind's eye or a coin in our hand, and so on. We see others in the same way: as first and foremost alive, moving and being moved to move.

Moreover we intuitively understand the movement of those around us. When we see an individual—human or nonhuman—lower itself before another, for example, we intuitively know it to be deferring in some way to the other. We intuitively understand because animate forms are indeed animate, and being animate they are kinesthetically attuned to the dynamics of their own movement, kinetically attuned to the visually experienced movement dynamics of others, and attuned in this double kinesthetic/kinetic sense to the relationship of the dynamics of their own movement to the movement dynamics of others. (For further readings on this topic, see Sheets-Johnstone 1994, 2008).

Ponderabilia 3:

ON BEHAVIOR AND MOVEMENT

The word "behavior" isn't up to capturing the dynamics of life itself. It wraps up the qualitative kinetic realities of movement in a word—or words—that completely veil the dynamics of ourselves as engaged living bodies, precisely as in the observation, "You're sawing wood" and in the answer "Yes, I'm sawing." It indeed does no more than put a label on a kinetic dynamic that is commonly both complex and subtle, complex in terms of a graduated force and pressure, for example, as in sawing wood, subtle in terms of shifts in attention, in lines of focus, and in weight-bearing legs. In short, behavior passes over the intricate drama of the main attraction.

Behaviorism was once the primary science in psychology. The science was initiated by John B. Watson who insisted that an objective science of living creatures, humans included, could be arrived at only through a study of what was concretely observable, namely, their overt behavior. What a human did at breakfast or in driving a car was no different from what a rat did in a maze: it responded to stimuli. From a behaviorist perspective, it is environmental stimuli that drive us all to do what we do; we are all biological machines, nothing more. Both human and nonhuman individuals are simply passive pieces of protoplasm that respond to whatever is out there in the environment in the form of a "stimulator."

Given behaviorist-savvy "stimulators," of course, the behavior of any individual can be predicted and controlled. The stimulator in charge can make anything out of anybody. An oft-quoted claim of Watson sums up the behaviorist's tenet: "Give me a dozen healthy infants, well-formed, and my own specified world to bring them up in and I'll guarantee to take any one at random and train him to become any type of specialist I might select—doctor, lawyer, artist, merchant-chief and yes, even beggar-man and thief, regardless of his talents, penchants, tendencies, abilities, vocations, and race of his ancestors" (Watson 1939, p. 104). Given this theoretical credo, it is evident that thoughts, emotions, motivations, mind, and consciousness count for naught. They are subjective, not objective, realities. Such subjective "entities" do not measure up—literally. They are not measurable according to the objective standards of science and are therefore outside its domain.

Psychologist B. F. Skinner (Burrhus Frederick Skinner) took up Watson's thesis and elaborated it along the lines of "operant conditioning," a process through which one could predict and control behavior through reinforcement, both positive and negative (Skinner 1974). Behaviorism in turn became the framework within which behavior modification therapy programs developed. Through various conditioning techniques—systematic desensitization, aversion, flooding—patients were "relieved" of their anxieties, their drug or alcohol addictions, and so on. Whether a matter of normal or abnormal behavior, behaviorism regarded humans as governed wholly by external stimuli and therefore as governable wholly by external stimuli. It is thus not too much to say that behaviorism roboticized life. It took the living steam out of experience along with abilities, native dispositions and motivations, and so on. Skinner in fact wrote, "I am a radical behaviorist simply in the sense that I find no place in the formulation for anything which is mental" (Skinner 1964, p. 106). It is notable, of course, that behaviorism in all its forms came to be broadly replaced by cognitive science—and cognitive therapy—a science Skinner dubbed "the creationism of psychology," emphatically rejecting and relegating to the fantasy dustbin any and all "internal unobservables" (R. I. Watson 1979, p. 392).

Though behaviorism gave way to cognitive science, behavior remains a paradigm of objective science and constitutes the subject matter of vast programs of human and nonhuman animal research. Even a modest amount of thought about animate life, however, reveals an essential insight. What emerges and evolves both ontogenetically and phylogenetically is fundamentally not behavior but movement. Eating, mating, nurturing, fighting, escaping, and so on, are all common and well-recognized behaviors in the animate world. What individualizes animals, however, both ontogenetically and phylogenetically, is their movement: how they move in doing what they do. In other words, while their movement may be neatly partitioned and classified as a certain behavior by an observer—eating, mating, or whatever—movement remains the basic phenomenon. Tactile-kinesthetic experience or corollaries thereof are primary in these real-life bodily happenings, for humans as for virtually all members of the animal kingdom. We may note that it takes time for some newborn creatures to learn their bodies and hone their movement. Humans especially are challenged first off and for some time to learn their bodies and learn to move themselves.

Tactile-kinesthetic experiences are basic to this learning. (For more on this topic, see Sheets-Johnstone 1999/2011.)

Shifting attention from behavior to movement, from the what to the how, clearly opens not just your eyes but your whole body to the realization that movement is not behavior. By extension, it opens not just your eyes but your whole body to the fact that what you experience in moving is not neurophysiological activity or neuron firings in your brain, but the qualitative dynamics of your own movement. To perceive others or yourself simply in terms of behavior indeed puts you on the outside of life as well as of yourself. You—and others—are simply an outer shell of "doings": eating, drinking, sleeping, shopping, parking, traveling. You name it—and you disappear! Remaining on the outside in this way, you fail to penetrate to the depths of your being, kinesthetically, affectively, and even cognitively.

When we turn away from behaviorist perspectives and become aware of our own movement, we open to our insides. Becoming aware of our own movement indeed de-roboticizes us—or at least puts us in the position of de-roboticizing. Opening to our insides sensitizes us to our moving body, our habits, our styles of moving, and most important, our possibilities not only of expanding our range of movement, for example, but of awakening our sense of aliveness.

Behavior is no match for experiencing and exploring our aliveness. Indeed, to view ourselves as reducible to our behaviors or to treat ourselves in behavior modification programs—a "tough-minded and pragmatic" approach to therapy that "conditions" people to change their behavior (Gleitman 1981, pp. 723-726)—is akin to reducing ourselves to our chemical makeup. As historian Herbert

Muller astutely observed: "To say . . . that a man is made up of certain chemical elements is a satisfactory description only for those who intend to use him as a fertilizer" (Muller 1943, p. 107).

Ponderabilia 4:

PULSING WITH LIFE!

Your movement pulse is not altogether different from the pulse your doctor takes when you go in for a check-up or for a diagnosis about an ailment. The doctor takes your pulse at your wrist—at what is called your radial pulse. But there are actually 20 places along the surface of your body—even more places, though some a bit more difficult to find than others—where you can feel your pulse. Your pulse is indeed an all-over body phenomenon! It reverberates throughout.

Your pulse reflects your heartbeat. It's coincident with the pumping of blood out of the left ventricle of your heart. That ejected blood goes all over your body. It's blood for general circulation. At points where arteries are close to the skin, you can feel your heart-beating pulse.

You can feel it at your temples (superficial temporal artery), for example, at either side of your jawbone (facial artery), at your trachea or windpipe (carotid artery), at the inside of your elbow (brachial artery), behind your knees (popiteal artery), and so on. Circulation of your blood throughout your body is obviously life-sustaining. In effect, movement of the heart in pumping blood is at the heart of life.

More than 2,500 years ago, Aristotle's intricate and extended studies of animals—human and nonhuman—led him to conclude that the heart is the source of all movement, including movement of the blood throughout the body. Aristotle in fact observed that "the pulse is perceptible by the senses wherever we touch the body" (482b17-18). His insights are truly remarkable. The soul of animals, he affirmed, has two faculties: the faculty of "discrimination which is the work of thought and sense," and the faculty of "originating local movement," that is, "forward movement" of an animal (432a15-17, 432b14). The heart is the centrepiece of both faculties: "life is always located in this part" (469a17).

In explaining his conclusion about the centrality of the heart, Aristotle states that "it is qua animal that a body is said to be a living thing, and it is called animal because endowed with sensation" (469a18-19). At the same time, however, an animal moves and it is the heart that is first of all moved, moved in what present-day biologists designate under the aegis of "responsivity" in their broad specification of life: "[p]lant seedlings bend toward the light; mealworms congregate in dampness; cats pounce on small moving objects; even bacteria move toward or away from particular chemicals" (Curtis 1975, p. 28). Aristotle rightly explains, "inasmuch as an animal is capable of appetite, it is capable of self-movement" (433b28-29). Appetites impel us to move. Desires are in other words felt and in this sense are affective aspects of corporeal life. Indeed, precisely as Aristotle observes, "affection is corporeal"; it resides in the body (453a14).

The examples Aristotle gives of affection in his treatise on memory are particularly striking in the present context. He writes, "remembering is the existence of a movement capable of stimulating the mind to the desired movement, and this . . . in such a way that the person should be moved from within himself, i.e., in consequence of movements wholly contained within himself" (452a10-13). Later, he writes that "bursts of anger or fits of terror, when once they have excited such motions [in the body] are not at once allayed, even though the angry or terrified persons set up counter motions, but the passions continue to move them on, in the same direction as at first. The affection resembles also that in the case of words, tunes, or sayings, whenever one of them has become inveterate on the lips. People give them up and resolve to avoid them; yet again and again they find themselves humming the forbidden air, or using the prohibited word" (453a27-31).

In short, affections of the soul stem from the heart. They are in Aristotelian terms "enmattered," which means that, in contrast to the common division of mind and body, animals—humans included—are all of a piece. That all-of-a-pieceness stems from the heart as the locus of body and soul: "All of the affections of soul involve a body—passion, gentleness, fear, pity, courage, joy, loving, and hating; in all these there is a concurrent affection of the body" (403a16-19). Following up on this thought that affections of the soul are "enmattered," Aristotle writes that in consequence, "anger should be defined as a certain mode of movement of such and such a body" (403a26-27). Moreover in his biological treatises on the parts of animals, he affirms again that "the motions of the body commence from the heart, and are brought about by traction and relaxation" (666b15-16). He adds, "The heart therefore . . . is as it were a living creature inside its possessor (666b16-17). In yet another treatise—this one on The Generation of Animals—he affirms that "the first principle of movement" arises from the heart" (735a25).

Aristotle's affirmations are clearly radical in today's mind/brain as well as mind/body divided world. They originate in real-life observations and resonate in experience rather than in theory or laboratory experiments. Because they do, they tie in in essential ways with what has been written here about your movement pulse.

Your movement pulse is also an all-over body phenomenon. The tightness or ease, expansiveness or constriction, weakness or strength with which you move is a tightness or ease throughout your body. When you turn attention to your own movement, you can feel its quality. Its dynamics are palpably present. In your determination to get something done and over with, you can be rushing and find a racing movement pulse, or you can be calm and composed and find an even-tempered pulse. You can obviously too be oblivious of any pulse whatsoever because you're simply not paying attention. Yet because you're alive, you're necessarily pulsing all over with life, whether aware of it or not! When you're aware of the dynamics that are at the heart of your life, you become correlatively aware of the movement prints you leave all about you.

Ponderabilia 5:

HOW COMMON MISUNDERSTANDINGS OF MOVEMENT OCCLUDE ITS QUALITATIVE REALITIES

Movement is commonly defined as a change of position or location. But does that definition make sense? Isn't it objects that change position? In other words, whatever the object—even a fork or spoon—it goes from point A to point B, then to point C, or back to point A, and so on.

The common understanding of movement in terms of an object veils over the qualitative realities of movement itself (Sheets-Johnstone 1979). When you notice movement and make differences that matter, those qualitative realities are precisely what come to the fore. You're noticing neither your transport from one point in space to another nor the time elapsed in the process of transport. What you're noticing are the dynamics of movement itself. In so doing, you come readily to the realization that movement—any movement—creates its own space, time, and force. It creates its own unique qualitative kinetic dynamic.

Think back in fact to your experience of a fully blown-up balloon being untied and then let loose. What does it do? It splutters about. The difference between experiencing the dynamics of movement itself and those of an object in motion is well exemplified, even epitomized, by just such an event. The movement of the untied balloon creates a recognizable qualitative kinetic dynamic. While the balloon is clearly an object in motion, what we experience in attending to what we verbally label "sputtering" is a vigorous, erratic, highly punctuated, wholly capricious flow of movement that ends in a sudden collapsing stillness. What captures our attention and is at the heart of our experience is not a balloon but movement. A particular qualitative kinetic dynamic unfolds before our eyes.

The movement of a leaf falling wispily to the ground is different from the movement of an untied balloon sputtering to the floor. What is the difference? The difference lies precisely in the kind of space and time the movement creates and the manner in which the kinetic force is projected. The falling leaf doesn't splutter any more than the balloon falls wispily. The tempo of movement is in each instance different; the spatial qualities of movement in terms of line and amplitude are equally different; and the energic quality of movement is in each instance different. In short, when we are attentive to movement itself, we experience a qualitative kinetic dynamic that is created by the movement itself.

The qualities of any kinetic dynamic are analyzable not simply in the broad terms of space, time, and force, but more specifically in terms of tensional quality, linear quality, areal quality, and projectional quality (Sheets-Johnstone 1966 [1979/1980], 1998, 1999/2011, 2009). Think of trudging up a steep hill. Your body is likely bent forward, your steps may be small, slow, and effortful, but at the same time even-paced and smooth. The tensional quality of movement is apparent in the intensity of effort or force you experience in trudging upward. The tensional quality may of course vary as you continue moving upward.

Where the incline is less steep, for example, you may spontaneously feel less effort and a greater ease in your movement.

The linear quality of your uphill climb has to do with the linear design of your moving body and the linear pattern of your movement. As suggested by the trudging character of a steep climb, the linear design of your body is likely diagonally inclined, tilted forward from the hips. The direction of your movement—the linear pattern the movement describes—likely proceeds in a straight line forward. But again, there may be, and likely are, variations. You may be hunched over at times along the way, thus curved rather than tilted diagonally forward, just as, at the opposite extreme, you may stretch to a full vertical alignment at times. Moreover with respect to linear pattern, it is not just your feet that are tracing out a linear pattern in a straight line forward, but your arms may be swinging forward and back. Further, if instead of looking continuously at the ground, you're looking alternately from one side to the other or you're looking up ahead and then down again, your moving head is tracing a quite distinct linear pattern. Then too, when you climb over or move sideways to avoid an obstacle in your path—a large broken tree limb or boulder—you definitively change both the linear design of your moving body and the linear pattern of your movement.

The areal quality of your uphill climb also has two components and is equally variable. The areal design of your body may be anywhere from small to large, contractive to expansive, precisely as in being hunched over as you climb or in being not only fully upright, but in swinging your arms in concert with your striding legs. Small, trudging steps make the areal pattern of your movement intensive; large, striding steps make it extensive. Amplitude is clearly a spatial dimension of any movement, specifying both the changing largeness and smallness of your moving body and the changing largeness and smallness of the movement itself.

Finally, projectional quality describes the manner in which effort or force is manifest: basically, in an abrupt, sustained, or ballistic manner. Trudging up a steep hill, you're likely moving in a sustained manner, plodding upward in an even, smooth gait. But you might also move sharply, for instance, in avoiding an unexpected overhanging branch, or begin swinging your arms in a ballistic manner, that is, with an initial impulse that carries the movement forward and then back through its own initially generated momentum. Your movement may indeed be a combination of different projectional qualities.

However brief, given the above qualitative analysis of movement, it should be clear why, contrary to popular thought and even to its common dictionary definition, movement is not a "change of position." The more attentive we are to the qualitative dynamics of our movement, the more apparent are the movement prints we leave about in moving. The prints trace out a spatio-temporal-energic dynamic that we might indeed come to recognize as uniquely our own in terms of a certain style of moving in doing the things we do in our everyday life.

We might incidentally note that movement as a change of position has a long history, tied to the notion of inertia and objects in motion. As Descartes stated, motion is "the transfer of one piece of matter, or one body, from the vicinity of the other bodies which are in immediate contact with it, and which are regarded as being at rest, to the vicinity of other bodies" (Descartes 1985 [1644], p. 233). If we are doing something like sitting down, lifting a suitcase, or cutting a swath of grass, point A and point B are typically the points of interest. They mark the place of departure and arrival of a moving body, and thereby the beginning and end of an aim or task. Points A and B, however, say nothing of the dynamics of movement. They describe a basically static spatial world intermittently interrupted by a body changing position.

Ponderabilia 6:

KINESTHETIC MEMORY

A famous Russian neuropsychologist, Alexander Romanovich Luria, esteemed for his meticulous clinical studies of his neurologically-afflicted patients and his equally meticulous studies of the brain, introduced the interchangeable descriptive terms "kinesthetic melody" and "kinetic melody." He used the terms to describe the flow of everyday patterns of movement in everyday life and their correlative neurological patterns of activity throughout the body (Luria 1966, 1973, 1980).

When we think of a melody, we think of a musical form that unfolds and that in the process of unfolding has certain contours: waxings and wanings, fortes and pianissimos, fullnesses and condensations of timbre, and so on. What Luria recognized in designating movement along the lines of a melody was precisely the equally qualitative nature of movement. It too unfolds, and in unfolding has certain contours: waxings and wanings, fortes and pianissimos, fullnesses and condensations, and so on. Whatever the movement, a certain qualitative dynamic flows forth.

When a musical melody is familiar, its dynamics are readily recognized. We listen; we know where we are in the piece and what comes next. The same is basically true of movement, but its truth comes with certain qualifications that have an added significance. If the dynamics of a movement are familiar—for example, if one is drying oneself after a shower or bath, or getting into one's car and putting the key in the ignition—they are commonly so familiar that they are in the background of one's awareness. One is not listening to them in the same way one listens to a familiar musical melody. In other words, when we are caught up in common everyday activities, we are commonly occupied elsewhere than in the movement itself. The dynamics—the kinesthetic melodies—run off by themselves as it were. But they do so because they are engrained in kinesthetic memory. Kinesthetic melodies are inscribed in our bodies. They are dynamic patterns of movement that constitute a basic, vast, and potentially ever-expandable repertoire of "I cans" (Husserl 1970, 1973, 1980, 1989) that permeates human life: walking, speaking, reaching, hugging, throwing carrying, brushing, opening, closing, running, wiping, pulling, pushing, and more.

The kinesthetic melody of drying oneself after a shower or of getting into one's car and putting the key in the ignition is a thoroughly familiar kinesthetic melody engrained in kinesthetic memory. Short of such a memory, we'd be perpetually at square one every moment of our lives, even when it comes to getting out of bed—or getting into it in the first place. Our primordial "I move" is there, but not an "I can." Whatever the kinesthetic melody might be, it comes from a background of learning our bodies and learning to move ourselves, which learnings allow us ultimately to be focally engaged elsewhere than in the movement at hand. (For more on kinesthetic memory, see Sheets-Johnstone 2003 and 2012.)

Philosophers—Martin Heidegger and John Searle are notable in this respect (Heidegger 1962, Searle 1992)—have regularly taken the everyday adult fact of being focally engaged elsewhere as the basis for their claim that one notices one's movement only when "something goes wrong." The "Background," as Searle names it, is otherwise opaque. As I elsewhere showed, however, "the belief that we know of the Background only when something goes wrong is an interesting but biased way of appreciating the Background. The belief effectively hides from us our own natality" (Sheets-Johnstone 1999, p. 249/2011, p. 215). In brief, we come into the world moving; we are precisely not stillborn. Coming into the world moving is the foundation upon which we learn our bodies and learn to move ourselves.

A further way of pointing up the import of our foundational or primal animation and its relationship to our learning our bodies and learning to move ourselves is to acknowledge the fact that "movement forms the I that moves before the I that moves forms movement" (ibid., pp. 137-138/p. 119). In other words, our natural, primal animation is the ground on which we learn to reach and grasp efficiently and effectively, on which we learn to stand by ourselves, on which we learn to walk and talk, on which we ultimately learn to do all those things we do in habitual or near-habitual ways as adult animate beings in the world.

To let kinesthetic memory go unrecognized is to take on an adultist stance, to pretend as if everything in what philosophers such as Heidegger and Searle call "the background" is a ready-made rather than a repertoire of acquired kinesthetic melodies. What is "in the background" is in truth a constellation of familiar movement patterns, what phenomenological philosopher Edmund Husserl terms "I cans," not only as in I can run, I can turn my head, I can thread the needle,

I can kick the ball, but as in I can calculate the distance, I can change directions, I can judge the size, and so on (Husserl 1989). All of our "I cans" are based on a prior capability, namely, "I move," just as that prior capability is based on our foundational or primal animation. Thus, the familiar patterns we move through, the kinesthetic melodies that make up our everyday life and that unfold regularly, are not in a background that remains opaque until "something goes wrong." They are the dynamically felt patterns of movement that have developed on the basis of our having learned our bodies and learned to move ourselves to begin with, and that have in turn become a staple of kinesthetic memory. Our everyday habits are indeed grounded in kinesthetic memory. They derive from kinesthetic experience and are neurologically structured in kinesthetic experience (Sheets-Johnstone 2003, 2009).

Luria gives a wonderfully detailed example of how a quite common kinetic melody is forged. He points out that "in the initial stages, writing depends on memorizing the graphic form of every letter. It takes place through a chain of isolated motor impulses, each of which is responsible for the performance of only one element of the graphic structure; with practice, this structure of the process is radically altered and writing is converted into a single 'kinetic melody,' no longer requiring the memorizing of the visual form of each isolated letter or individual motor impulses for making every stroke" (Luria 1973, p. 32).

In sum, anytime we care to pay attention to our kinesthetic melodies, there they are: throwing, carrying, wiping, leaping, pulling, speaking, writing . . . our kinesthetic repertoire of melodies is virtually limitless, being constrained only by age, inclination—and pathology.

It is important to emphasize that kinesthetic melodies are not just patterns of "know-how." They are not "merely physical." They are saturated in cognitive and affective acuities that anchor movement invariants. They are indeed saturated in knowledge, in a kinetic bodily logos that is alert, attentive, and discriminating, that distinguishes and judges in the course of moving, for example. At the same time, they are saturated in cognitive and affective ways that individualize the manner in which any particular melody runs off, that color the particular way in which it habitually unfolds. Invariants are thus dynamically tailored qualitatively to the situation of the moment.

We move or tend to move within our own accustomed qualitative dynamics. But as putting movement into your life shows, we can surprise ourselves. We can, as it were, edit our dynamics such that what we do has a new felt verve and sense about it. We readily have the option of doing so. While melody and memory are dynamic images of one another—"integral kinesthetic structures," as Luria terms melodies (Luria 1973, p. 176)—they are malleable. What is familiar is open to exploration; what is inscribed is not indelibly inscribed. It depends on our attitude, on our zest for play, on our willingness to tap into our primal animation, stretch the boundaries of our habitual movement, and transform our habits into stepping stones toward an invigorated life. We are never too old to invent new dynamics or to change old ones. We are never too old to reinvigorate kinesthetic memory.

Ponderabilia 7:

THE GIFT OF PLAY

Being an adult is being serious. Being an adult means leaving play behind, doing real work, accomplishing what's important. But leaving play behind or being deprived of play are serious life deficits. On the basis of both state-sponsored legal investigations and evolutionary studies, psychiatrist Stuart Brown has shown in eloquent and unequivocal ways that play matters.

Brown was on the 1960 panel charged by then governor of Texas, John Connally, to determine the kind of childhood experiences that led Charles Whitman to mass murder people as they climbed to a tower situated on a university campus. In his summation of the case for the governor, Brown wrote, "We had originally expected to discover a brain tumor and drugs as primary causal agents, but our intensive investigation weighted abuse and playlessness as the major factors placing him and his future victims at risk" (Brown 1998, p. 248). An article of Brown's in *National Geographic* (1994) testifies further to the importance of play and to the fact that it is a natural proclivity of many, many species of animals.

As I have elsewhere shown, where competition drowns out play, it drowns out laughter; it drowns out explorations of one's own capacity to move; it drowns out the possibility of thinking creatively in movement. When competition prematurely obscures the significance of play for young children and belittles its significance for adults as well, the damage is correlatively doubled (Sheets-Johnstone 2003, 2008).

Playing isn't just for the young. It's for adolescents, young adults, middle-aged folks, and older people. It is there at hand and more for everyone. One has only to acknowledge it and cultivate its never-ending possibilities. People who can't grasp the pleasure others find in bodily play may well be out of touch with their own bodies, experiencing them only in a kind of third-person way, like the main character—James Duffy—in a short story by James Joyce. Mr. James Duffy, Joyce writes, "lived at a little distance from his body, regarding his own acts with doubtful side-glances." Not only this, but "he had an odd autobiographical habit which led him to compose in his mind from time to time a short sentence about himself containing a subject in the third person and a predicate in the past tense" (Joyce 1947, p. 119). The title of the short story is actually "A Painful Case." A painful case indeed! Persons living at a distance from their bodies are out of touch with the kinetic joyride that movement affords (Sheets-Johnstone 1986, p. 242; 2003, p. 416; 2009, p. 87).

Charles Darwin implicitly recognizes play in his study of emotions in human and nonhuman animals, specifically in the context of his observations of joy and pleasure. He points out that "under a transport of Joy or of vivid Pleasure, there is a strong tendency to various purposeless movements, and to the utterance of various sounds." It is clear from his ongoing observations that "purposeless movements" and "various sounds" are neither trivial nor meaningless. They are found, he writes, "in our young children, in their loud laughter, clapping of hands, and jumping for joy; in the bounding and barking of a dog when going out to walk with his master, and in the frisking of a horse when turned out into an open field. Joy quickens the circulation, and stimulates the brain, which again reacts on the whole body" (Darwin 1965 [1872], p. 76). Moreover he goes on to observe that "with animals of all kinds, the acquirement of almost all their pleasures, with the exception of those of warmth and rest, are associated, and have long been associated with active movement" (ibid., p. 77).

The laughter that comes with human play has evolutionary ties with the movement and sounds made by other primates in play. As ethologist J. A. R. A. M. van Hooff has shown, human laughter has "a great similarity in form with the relaxed open-mouth face" of catarrhine (Old World) monkeys and apes, "especially in connection with the rhythmic, low-pitched staccato vocalizations and the boisterous body movements" that accompany their facial expression (van Hooff 1969, p. 77; see also van Hooff 1972). Darwin in fact had earlier observed that tickling elicits a similar response in chimpanzees and humans: "If a young chimpanzee be tickled—and the armpits are particularly sensitive to tickling, as in the case of our children, . . . [a] chuckling or laughing sound is uttered; though the laughter is sometimes noiseless. The corners of the mouth are . . . drawn backwards; and this sometimes causes the lower eyelids to be slightly wrinkled. But this wrinkling, which is so characteristic of our own laughter, is more plainly seen in some monkeys" (Darwin 1965 [1872], p. 131).

What the above observations lead us to conclude if we are willing to follow them is that the practicalities of adulthood and the responsibilities that come with them are bound to be drudgerous only insofar as we doom ourselves to drudgery. We are free to play. Play is indeed a gift that is there for us anytime we choose to acknowledge it and open ourselves to its bounties. It comes with our very aliveness, with our being the moving bodies we are.

Social anthropologists Tim Ingold and Jo Lee Vergunst point out that whether a matter of doing, thinking, or speaking, "everything takes place, in one way or the other, on the move" (Ingold and Vergunst 2008, p. 3). We easily tend to overlook that "everything" does. Indeed, when we think, we move things thoughtfully along: we follow through on a line of thought and move ourselves as well as our ideas around with bodily feelings of conviction, excitement, doubt, and so on, and these feelings are not uncommonly accompanied by nods, smiles, grimaces, vacant stares, frowns, and the like. We also, of course, at times come to a dead stop. But we often also play with ideas. We toss them about, bundle them off here and there, try them out on others, and in the course of doing so gesture in bodily ways, to this side and that, expansively and contractively, vigorously and hesitantly, explosively and dawdlingly, and in all subtle and complex possibilities between. Movement is part of our discourse as well as our thinking.

Dictionaries tell us that child's play is "something that is easily done." True enough in the sense that it flows forth spontaneously, that is, it comes naturally; but untrue to the core in suggesting that it is thereby of little merit.

Child's play is in fact the original sport. It is there before any cultural or developmental shifts toward competition and dominance. It constitutes a kinetic engagement with one's own body—and the bodies of others—that is great fun. It can also at times generate fear in varying degrees by bringing vulnerabilities to the fore, vulnerabilities that come with an awareness of the possibility of being hurt, an awareness of one's own basic fragility. The kind of play of moment here, however, is vulnerability-free, or virtually so. The only risk in allowing yourself the "transport of joy" and "vivid pleasure" that come with play might be in feeling silly. But to paraphrase Shakespeare, if such joy and pleasure be the food of life, move on!

Ponderabilia 8:

ON CREATIVITY, WONDER, AND THE UNSUNG KINETIC IMAGINATION

One doesn't have to be an artist to be creative. Consider, for example, the juvenile chimpanzee who invented his own invitation to play. Rather than going through the ritualized motions of the "play-hitting" gesture, in which an individual raises an arm overhead with respect to another individual (as if intending to hit him or her) and then waits for the other to respond by initiating play, this juvenile chimpanzee initiated play "by presenting a limp leg to another individual as it passed by (an invitation to grab it and so initiate a game of chase), looking back and forth between the recipient and its leg in the process" (Tomasello and Call 1997, p. 244).

To be creative means basically to think outside habitual or traditional ways of doing. It means being willing to be at the doorstep of the unknown, on the brink, on the edge. Philosopher Eugen Fink captured the essence of this terra incognita experience when he wrote about wonder. Wonder, he said, "dislodges man from the prejudice of everyday, publicly pregiven, traditional and worn out familiarity . . . drives him from the already authorized and expressly explicated interpretation of the sense of the world and into the creative poverty of not yet knowing" (Fink 1981, p. 24).

Fink's words actually echo those of Leonardo da Vinci who, 400 years earlier, described his experience in face of a great cavern: "Urged on by my eagerness to see the many varied and strange forms shaped by artful nature, I wandered for some time among the shady rocks and finally came to the entrance of a great cavern. At first I stood before it dumbfounded, knowing nothing of such a thing; then I bent over with my left hand braced against my knee and my right shading my squinting, deep-searching eyes; again and again I bent over, peering here and there to discern something inside; but the all-embracing darkness revealed nothing. Standing there, I was suddenly struck by two things, fear and longing: fear of the dark ominous cavern; longing to see if inside there was something wonderful" (da Vinci 1959, p. 19).

Like other forms of animate life, we humans are understandably leery of trying something new. Indeed, emotions and movement go hand in hand: they are dynamically congruent. Fear moves us to move in ways different from longing in the same way that it moves us to move in ways different from trust (Sheets-Johnstone 1999, 2006, 2008). What is familiar and unfamiliar resonate in bodily felt ways. Da Vinci's descriptive account of the opposing bodily-felt inclinations of fear and longing resonates with the two sides of wonder that oftentime grip us in face of unknowns in the present-day world about us.

But wonder can come not only with respect to "the sense of the world" or to "artful nature." It can come with respect to movement, the life-breath of one's own being and aliveness. When such wonder takes hold, all sorts of creative explorations are possible—and all sorts of hesitations may arise. To begin with, though, one doesn't simply decide to be creative and to invent something new. One simply recognizes one's freedom to imagine possibilities of doing otherwise, not recklessly, but attentively, with utmost kinesthetic awareness of the new and fresh dynamics one can create or is creating. It is from and with this kinesthetically charged awareness that one's kinetic imagination can run loose.

To be aware of new and fresh dynamics is actually to be more focally and acutely aware of the old ones, those ordinary, familiar dynamics that inform everyday life. When someone asks you your name, for example, you reply with a sequence of familiar sounds, a sequence that has certain accents and pauses running through it. The same is true in writing your name, whether in formal fashion as on a license or legal paper of some kind or in pro forma fashion as with a quick signature. If you write your name in the air without a pencil and on a pretend piece of paper, you'll notice with greater attention the qualitative kinetic dynamics that structure your name-writing movement. You'll notice the dynamics even more acutely if you write your name in the empty space in front of you with eyes closed.

Any qualitative kinetic dynamic has a particular dynamic line, in just the same way that nursery rhymes—"Mary Had a Little Lamb," "Hickory Dickory Dock," and "Baa, Baa, Black Sheep"—have particular dynamic lines (Sheets-Johnstone 1966 [1979/1980]). The lines may be vocalized in nonsense syllables, as in the first two syllables of "Baa ,Baa, Black Sheep." When we recite the latter rhyme, the vocal intensity of each "baa" is moderately strong. If we increase the intensity, making each "baa" more potent, we can feel a stronger tension in our throat and elsewhere through our body. We can in fact come up with a vigorous and explosive "Baa! Baa!," or perhaps better written "Bah! Bah!" Alternatively, we can keep the first syllable as usually uttered and change only the second one, or vice versa; we can inhale instead of exhale as we utter either syllable and furthermore attenuate its projection. In short, we can make all manner of gradation in the rhyme's qualitative kinetic dynamics.

Striking out anew in such ways brings endless creative possibilities of movement to life. Playing around with these possibilities brings you to life along with the possibilities. It brings you to life by summoning the creative powers of your imagination and by giving your kinetic imagination free rein. As Theseus observes in Shakespeare's *A Midsummer Night's Dream* (Act 5, Scene 1), imagination "bodies forth the form of things unknown." In this instance, imagination bodies forth your moving body, a 'you' previously submerged in habitual doings, forms of life that were void of your imaginative input and didn't draw on your creative powers.

In this strongly cognitive and information-driven age in which we live, the value as well as the power of our creative imagination can go virtually unrecognized. Our creative play, however, can begin with something as simple as a sneeze. We can first of all become aware that each and every sneeze has a particular dynamic line. When we sneeze and become aware of its unique dynamics, we can in turn realize that we have the possibility of recreating those dynamics in whatever total bodily movement way we like.

Creative play can indeed begin with whatever is arising—whatever that may be. Becoming aware of the dynamics of one's own everyday movement—be it voluntary like putting on your pants or involuntary like a sneeze—one plumbs creative possibilities and to whatever depths one wishes.

The words of psychoanalyst Carl Jung on the commonly overlooked value of the imagination are inspiring to recall in just this context. Jung wrote, "For everyone whose guiding principle is adaptation to external reality, imagination is for these reasons something reprehensible and useless. And yet we know that every good idea and all creative work are the offspring of the imagination, and have their source in what one is pleased to call infantile fantasy. Not the artist alone, but every creative individual whatsoever owes all that is greatest in his life to fantasy. The dynamic principle of fantasy is play, a characteristic also of the child, and as such it appears inconsistent with the principle of serious work. But without this playing with fantasy no creative work has ever yet come to birth. The debt we owe to the play of imagination is incalculable" (Jung 1976, p. 63).

Ponderabilia 9:

THOUGHTS ABOUT SPACE, MOTORS— AND MORE!

A common understanding of movement is true: movement does take place in space. An airplane jets across the sky; an ant crawls along the ground; traffic inches its way at rush hour. Whatever is moving, its movement can indeed be seen as taking place in space. Moreover its movement takes place in time. Movement is in fact commonly defined as a force in time and space: we can measure the distance traveled across the sky, along the ground, and at rush hour; we can measure the amount of force involved in the travel; and we can measure the time involved. Whatever the movement, it is definitely a force of some kind that takes place in space and time. We see it! And seeing is believing!

The problem comes in believing only in what is seen.

A fine and telling example of the problem comes from philosopher Daniel Dennett, who, in writing about lobsters and other animals (animals he may only have seen on his plate), differentiates their activities from "the sorts of sophisticated activities human bodies engage in," activities in which he says "there are more options, and hence more sources of confusion." As far as a lobster is concerned, Dennett says, "Its options are limited, and when it 'thinks of' moving a claw, its 'thinker' is directly and appropriately wired to the very claw it thinks of moving" (Dennett 1991, p. 427). The situation is different in humans, Dennett says, because "the body's control system (housed in the brain) has to be able to recognize a wide variety of different sorts of inputs as informing it about itself, and when quandaries arise or scepticism sets in, the only reliable (but not foolproof) way of sorting out and properly assigning this information is to run little experiments: do something and look to see what moves" (ibid., pp. 427-28).

We are back at square one. Kinesthesia is nowhere on the map. We would indeed be hard put if we had to "do something and look to see what moves" in order to inform ourselves about ourselves—as if our human "thinker" was not also "directly and appropriately wired" to our human body.

In myriad ways, kinesthesia constitutes and informs our everyday lives. In behavioral terms, it constitutes and informs our eating, driving, sitting, standing, and talking; in richly dynamic movement terms, it constitutes and informs our reaching, twisting, bending, pushing away, pulling up, putting down, stretching, turning, throwing, kicking, walking, balancing, opening, closing, and so much more.

When you take any one of these movements in the context of its actual happening, you become aware that your movement doesn't simply take place in space, but creates its own space. That it does so in part explains the familiar spatial dynamics that inform your everyday movements: the spatial dynamics in your stooping to pick up a dropped napkin from the floor; the spatial dynamics in your throwing a ball to a young child as distinct from your throwing the ball to an adult. In the latter instance, your throwing movement is not only likely more forceful and faster; it is also of greater amplitude and likely carves a higher and greater arc or linear pattern. To appreciate spatial dynamics and their differences means to experience movement itself. In experiencing movement itself, you realize that you create dynamic spatial forms in the very process of moving. You realize in turn that movement does not simply take place in space—and in time. Movement creates a certain spatiality—and temporality—as part of its overall kinetic dynamic.

The visual often swamps the kinesthetic. Pick up any textbook on physiology or psychology and you will find not just one, but often several chapters on vision—and on hearing—and little if anything on kinesthesia or proprioception. Other oversights and even oddities are apparent as well. In a textbook on movement, for example, in a chapter on "The Proprioceptors and Their Associate Reflexes," physiologists Barbara Gowitzke and Morris Milner state, "The voluntary contribution to movement is almost entirely limited to initiation, regulation of speed, force, range, and direction, and termination of the movement" (Gowitzke and Milner 1988, p. 193). Their way of putting the matter is negative because their central focus is on what is neurophysiologically transpiring in self-movement. All the same, their straightforward acknowledgment of range and direction—distinctly spatial aspects of human movement, specifically areal and linear qualities—leaves no doubt but that movement is inherently spatial, that range and direction are experienced, and that being experienced, they are open to experiential investigations and creative explorations.

The very notion of human movement having "degrees of freedom," as highly revered physiologist Nicolas Bernstein first demonstrated (Bernstein 1984), is in fact testimonial to what is virtually an expanse of kinesthetic possibilities.

The practice of "motorizing" animate movement and the seeming fascination with a 'motorology' (Sheets-Johnstone 2003, 2009a, 2009b, 2012) are further oddities. In no less than *The Cambridge Handbook of Consciousness*, and in no less than a chapter therein titled "Consciousness and Control of Action," a chapter in which we would rightfully expect to find a discussion of kinesthesia and proprioception, we find the following near-opening statement: "In the present chapter, I am concerned exclusively with motor (i.e., bodily) actions" (Umiltà 2007, p. 327).

What kind of body could this be? Surely not an animate body alive in a world that is never quite the same from one moment to the next and that requires in the most basic evolutionary sense a mindful body capable of making its way successfully in a changing world.

Clearly, and especially in a book on consciousness, motorologists would do well to wean themselves away from sensory-motor talk and work toward languaging the realities of sensory-kinetic/kinesthetic experience. Twenty-five hundred years ago, Aristotle observed, "Nature is a principle of motion and change." He concluded, "We must therefore see that we understand what motion is; for if it were unknown, nature too would be unknown" (200b12-14). Surely we would all do well to heed Aristotle's call.

We would do well too to heed Darwin, whose extended and painstakingly detailed observations of animate life around the world gave him insights into Nature that resonate with special force in much of today's tunnel-visioned sightings on the brain. Darwin's estimation of the philosophically, psychologically, and neuroscientifically vexed relationship of mind and body, of the challenge the relationship presents, and of the proper mode of conceiving and approaching the challenge are of decisive moment to consider. Darwin wrote, "Experience shows the problem of the mind cannot be solved by attacking the citadel itself.—the mind is function of body.—we must bring some stable foundation to argue from" (Darwin 1987 [1838], p. 564). Surely animation is the stable foundation, for animation is inclusive of the whole of animate life and is thus integral to all-inclusive and penetrating understandings of Nature.

The moral: when heads roll, everything feels it because everything is part of Nature, and in Nature, everything is connected to everything else.

Ponderabilia 10:

IN THE BEGINNING . . .

As noted in Ponderabilia 6, in the beginning, "movement forms the I that moves before the I that moves forms movement." Our sense of agency thus derives from movement. In his book *Acts of Meaning*, child psychologist Jerome Bruner emphasizes how, in language development, an infant's interest centers on "agentivity," that is, on the moving body as agent and on self-movement in relation to objects (Bruner 1990, pp. 77-78). The acts of meaning he describes may be more finely limned as synergies of meaningful movement, synergies that have in fact been developing from the beginning, that is, from the time an infant is born and comes to realize its capacity to turn over, to make effective reaching movements, to grasp and to let go, not to mention its later capacity to walk and talk (Sheets-Johnstone 2009, 2012).

While not designed toward showing the natural bond between agency and movement, an experiment conducted by infant psychiatrist and clinical psychologist Daniel Stern provides a striking validation of the bond (Stern 1985). Stern's experiment was with Siamese twins prior to the operation that separated them at four months of age.

The twins were joined between navel and sternum. The experiment consisted in determining any difference in the bodily movement of the twins when they were deterred from sucking their own fingers and when they were deterred from sucking the fingers of their twin. When the twin's own arm was pulled away from her mouth by a researcher—the pulling movement resulting in the twin's own fingers being pulled out of her mouth—the twin resisted the pull: she attempted to pull her own arm back toward herself. When her twin's arm was pulled away from her mouth by a researcher—the pulling movement resulting in her twin's fingers being pulled out of her mouth—the twin strained her head forward in pursuit of the retreating fingers, that is, in pursuit of something alien to her own body. In documenting two distinctively different bodily movements, the experiment documents both a bodily sense of self in the form of a tactile-kinesthetic body and a bodily sense of self-agency.

Throughout his writings, phenomenological philosopher Edmund Husserl recognized the import of agency in what he termed "I cans." This fundamental and eminently significant "faculty," as Husserl termed it, can hardly be ignored. One's repertoire of "I cans" constitutes the span of one's "agentivity" not merely in the sense of physical prowess or achievements, but in the broad sense of one's wisdom of oneself and the lifeworld one inhabits. As Husserl remarks, "I can draw conclusions, compare, distinguish, connect, count, calculate; also, I can evaluate and weigh values," and so on. In other words, it is not only that "I can" play the piano or draw a horse, but that "I can" remember, think, and imagine. A faculty, Husserl thus reminds us, "is not an empty ability but is a positive potentiality, which may now happen to be actualized but which is always in readiness to pass into activity" (Husserl 1989, pp. 266-67).

160

"I cans" are thus both accomplishments and portals opening onto possibilities yet to be realized. Whatever their form—a jump, reach, and fall in catching a ball; a series of thoughts or memories; a series of pirouettes; a concluding judgment—they originate in movement of some order. That is, originally, the experience "I move" precedes the conceptual realization "I can do," which is precisely to say that "movement forms the I that moves before the I that moves forms movement." Movement is thus foundational not only to perceptual realizations of ourselves as doing or accomplishing certain things or making certain things happen, and to correlative cognitive realizations of ourselves as capable of just such acts or activities, but to our perceptual-cognitive-affective realization of ourselves as alive, that is, as living creatures, animate organisms, animate forms of life.

Fundamental human concepts actually derive from bodily experiences, experiences of our own bodies, their movement and their dynamics (Sheets-Johnstone 1990, 2008). Any creature's corporeal consciousness is in fact first and foremost a consciousness attuned to the movement and rest of its own body. Spiders, insects, and other forms of invertebrate life are proprioceptively aware of the world about them and move in ways appropriate to their awarenesses. Their external proprioceptive sensory organs have names: slit sensilla, campaniform sensilla, lyriform organs, and so on. All are in the service of "surface recognition sensitivity" (Sheets-Johnstone 1998, 1999/2011). As one invertebrate researcher writes, "proprioceptive information plays a vital part in the control of movements and orientation" (Lissman 1950, p. 35). In short, any creature that moves itself senses itself moving. By the same token, it senses when it is still. In effect, a corporeal consciousness is a dimension of living forms that move themselves, that are animate.

Both kinesthesia and proprioception are evolutionary facts of life. Proprioception is the more general term specifying not only a sense of position and movement but a sense of balance, gravitational orientation, and tactility. As its etymology indicates, kinesthesia refers specifically to a sense of movement. Hence, in its primary, i.e., experiential, sense, it denotes an awareness of a spatio-temporal-energic dynamics and thus an awareness of a qualitatively felt kinetic flow. When we awaken to the kinesthetically-endowed living bodies we are, we awaken precisely to the flow of our movement, to the dynamic intricacies and subtleties of our own animation.

Given their joint evolutionary heritage, we might ask precisely how, in an evolutionary sense, kinesthesia relates to proprioception. Invertebrate researcher M. S. Laverack (Laverack 1976) has shown—and others by their research suggest—that external proprioceptive organs were internalized over time to form an internally sensitive corporeal consciousness, what we may rightly term a basically kinesthetic rather than tactile consciousness, and this by way of a musculature attached to an articulable skeleton (for more on this topic, see Sheets-Johnstone 1998, 1999/2011). Kinesthesia gives us a direct and immediate sense of our own movement through sensory organs in our muscles, tendons, and joints. External proprioceptive organs are, as indicated, in the service of surface recognition sensitivity: a spider feels vibrations on its web when a fly or other insect lands on it; a locust is proprioceptively sensitive to air currents and adjusts its flight and orientation accordingly. Like other mammals, we humans are proprioceptively as well as kinesthetically endowed, not only in terms of gravitation and balance, but specifically in terms of tactility, that is, in terms of surface recognition sensitivity: when we flex our arms or legs, we touch ourselves, forearm meeting upper arm at our elbow joint, foreleg meeting upper leg at our knee joint.

We can indeed trace the evolution of a corporeal consciousness by way of proprioception and kinesthesia. In doing so, we have the possibility of coming to deepened appreciations of movement, which is to say of the inherent kinetic nature of life, and in turn, the kinetic proclivities, spontaneities, and possibilities of animate forms of life.

Ponderabilia 11:

SYNERGIES OF MEANINGFUL MOVEMENT

Synergies of meaningful movement abound in everyday life. The synergies are undergirded by qualitative kinetic dynamics, dynamics so familiar that they run off by themselves. It is not that you go through the motions of this or that task like a robot. On the contrary, your mindful body is already kinesthetically attuned to the task such that the synergies involved simply flow forth.

At one time, however, you learned the movement that now runs off by itself. You learned to tie a shoelace; you learned to brush your teeth. In the course of such learning, you became familiar not simply with a certain pattern of movement—now this, now this, now this—but with an overall dynamic flow. What you experienced then was not a sensation here and a sensation there, or even a sequence of sensations here and there. You experienced a particular space-time-force qualitative dynamic.

The distinction between sensations and dynamics is critical to understanding how synergies of meaningful movement develop and formally evolve (Sheets-Johnstone 2006). Just as there is a decisive experiential and descriptive difference between behavior and movement, so there is a decisive experiential and descriptive difference between sensations and dynamics.

While many people—even dancers—speak of kinesthetic sensations, they mislead us about the realities of kinesthetic experience. Sensations are spatially localized and temporally punctual. They are discrete bodily-sensed events like an itch, a flash of light, a blast of hot air, a shove, a pinprick, a peppery taste, a jolting halt, and so on. While the sensational experience might be repeated—a second flash of light or jolting halt, for example—its repetition does not change its temporally punctual and spatially localized character.

Sensations can certainly coalesce to form either a kinetic perception or an affective feeling, however, as when, for example, in experiencing a throbbing sensation, we attend not to each sensation by itself, but to the ongoing steady pulse of the throbbing and perceive a recurrent rhythm and hence a temporal continuity, or to the ongoing agony and distress of the throbbing and feel the relentless and unremitting character of the pain and hence an affective continuity. The sensations themselves do not change, but our consciousness of them changes.

Given the discrete experiential nature of sensations, the problem with "kinesthetic sensations" becomes obvious. In walking down the street, opening our arms to greet a friend, or sitting down in a chair, we do not experience our movement as a series of moment-by-moment, now-here, now-here happenings: we have neither spatially pointillist and temporally punctual kinesthetic sensations nor coalescing sensations as described above. We have kinesthetic feelings of a particular qualitative kinetic dynamic.

Imagine, for example, that you have picked up your toothbrush, opened your mouth, and are about to put your brush in your mouth and brush your teeth. Imagine, however, that someone comes in, takes your toothbrush from you, puts it in your mouth and brushes your teeth. You would immediately recognize that you yourself were not brushing your teeth, not simply because someone took your brush from you and because you see that someone now standing before you holding your toothbrush, but because you would definitively feel a foreign dynamics inside your mouth!

Synergies of meaningful movement are the product of sense-making in a double sense (Sheets-Johnstone 2009a, 2009b). When as infants we learn our bodies and learn to move ourselves, we make sense of both our core animacy, the moving bodies we are, and of our capacity to move sensibly, that is, effectively and efficiently in the world generally and in the world of other animate beings. In the process, we forge fundamental human concepts, nonlinguistic corporeal-kinetic concepts such as round, in, inside, open, under, straight, bent, and so on (Sheets-Johnstone 1990, 1994, 1999, 2008, 2009a). Our double sense-makings are epistemologically rooted in these concepts. In learning our bodies and learning to move ourselves, we progressively make more and more sense of ourselves, that is, we explore and come to know the world in moving about in it, drawing closer to touch something, bending over to inspect an underside, and so on. Correlatively, we make progressively more and more sense of the world about us, that is, we forge and attain meanings in the course of realizing our possibilities of movement—reaching for and grasping something we want to play with, closing our mouth and turning our head away to avoid being fed a food we do not want, and so on. We make sense of ourselves and the world through movement. We make sense in both senses, creating synergies of meaningful movement.

In essence, then, a semantic congruency obtains in the relationship between movement and meaning (Sheets-Johnstone 1990, 1994, 1999,

2004, 2009b). Whatever our particular bodily-kinetic dynamic, it is meaningfully motivated and our movement articulates that meaning. We thereby create the manifold synergies of meaningful movement that inform our everyday lives. We create new synergies when we learn to play tennis or to make surgical incisions. An infant learning to walk is kinesthetically feeling its way into a synergy of meaningful movement. Children playing together are creating synergies of meaningful movement. Two friends greeting each other and individuals shaking hands on meeting for the first time are doing the same: they are engaging in complementary synergies of meaningful movement informed by a dynamic and semantic congruency.

Social synergies of meaningful movement are not necessarily all sweetness and light. In a heated argument, for example, synergies of meaningful movement are antagonistic: "You did this!" "No, I didn't—you did it!"; or "You said X!" "But you said Y first!"; and so on. The unfolding verbal interchanges themselves feed into and escalate the dynamics. In effect, whether friendly or antagonistic, individuals involved in social synergies of meaningful movement are not simply moving through a form, going through the motions as it were. The form is moving through them, affecting, propelling, and even empowering or disempowering them every step of the way, and in a whole-body manner that includes not just the words they articulate but the dynamics of those so-called "articulatory gestures."

Human tongues are waggable, not in the same way that dogs' tails are waggable—human tongues are waggable in far more complex ways, including being mis-waggable—but their dynamic patternings, their synergies of meaningful movement, are as unmistakable as the synergies of the whole-body dynamic of which a dog's tail is a part.

Ponderabilia 12:

ON THE TEMPORALITY OF OUR ALIVENESS

In this speeded-up age in which we live, waiting is commonly considered a waste of time. But it may also envelop us in an emotional dynamic of some kind—a dynamic of agitation, of tensed-up worry, or of the quite different dynamic of boredom. Our affective and kinetic dynamics are indeed congruent (Sheets-Johnstone 1999, 2008). In other words, what we feel emotionally and kinesthetically is of a piece. If our affective and kinesthetic feelings were not experientially intertwined, there would be no possibility of feigning an emotion by moving through its kinetic dynamics, or of inhibiting the kinetic expression of an emotion. The dual possibilities attest unmistakably to the fact that an emotion may be corporeally experienced even though not carried forth into movement, or it may be mimed but not actually experienced.

Martin Heidegger, an existential philosopher noted for his complex metaphysics of human being, wrote a surprisingly concise and exacting description of boredom at a train station at the beginning of his quest to understand boredom, what he termed "profound boredom," the "fundamental attunement" of human being (of *Dasein*). His descriptive account, titled "Passing the Time As a Driving Away of Boredom That Drives Time On," begins as follows:

> We are sitting, for example, in the tasteless station of some lonely minor railway. It is four hours until the next train arrives. The district is uninspiring. We do have a book in our rucksack, though—shall we read? No. Or think through a problem, some question? We are unable to. We read the timetables or study the table giving the various distances from this station to other places we are not otherwise acquainted with at all. We look at the clock—only a quarter of an hour has gone by. Then we go out onto the local road. We walk up and down, just to have something to do. But it is no use. Then we count the trees along the road, look at our watch again—exactly five minutes since we last looked at it. Fed up with walking back and forth, we sit down on a stone, draw all kinds of figures in the sand, and in so doing catch ourselves looking at our watch again—half an hour—and so on (Heidegger 1995, p. 93).

At a train station—or at an airport—it's not something in particular that we find boring. It's that in waiting, we are confronted by seemingly endless time: it seems to be standing still. Yet obviously, it's not time that's standing still; it's we who are standing still in time. Our stillness in waiting calls attention to time. Time is passing and life feels empty.

When we turn time on our hands into movement or into an attention to movement, there is no more time on our hands. We can marvel at the effortless rising and falling of breath. We can become engrossed in some aspect of our aliveness: where do we feel our breath? in our nostrils? chest? abdomen? We can feel the heaviness of a relaxed lower jaw, the unvarying evenness of our heartbeats, the incredible swiftness of blinking that fails to interrupt the continuity of the visual scene before us, or the intricate movements of swallowing. Our insides are alive in subtle, complex, and altogether spontaneous ways. Life is indeed on the move inside and out.

Moreover our flesh itself is alive to movement. Simple, mundane experiences attest to the living realities of flesh. As philosopher Jean-Paul Sartre observed, when my body is no longer experienced as an instrument, but lived as flesh, then I experience objects in the world as flesh: "A contact with them is a caress; that is, my perception is not the utilization of the object. . . . I discover something like a flesh of objects. My shirt rubs against my skin, and I feel it. What is ordinarily for me an object most remote becomes the immediately sensible; the warmth of air, the breath of the wind, the rays of sunshine, etc.; all are present to me in a certain way . . . revealing my flesh by means of their flesh" (Sartre 1956, p. 392).

It seems only proper in this context to recognize Edmund Husserl again, a philosopher whose seminal phenomenological investigations and detailed descriptions of human experience launched existential philosophy and philosophers such as Heidegger and Sartre along new paths. Husserl wrote of the body as the "zero-point of orientation," the "here" of any experienced "there." He wrote about the ways in which we go from the sensuous presence of things to meanings and values, what he called "the constitution of objects." He wrote about the dual, intermeshed systems of the sensorial and the motional, or the perceptual and "the kinestheses," that is, how by obtaining different "profiles" of objects in moving about, we come to "constitute" the objects as meant: we put the profiles—our different perspectival experiences of things—together as chairs, trees, houses, and so on, objects that are distinctively meaningful to us. He wrote about empathy and how it grounds our intersubjective world. And he wrote at length about temporality in terms of internal time consciousness through which past and future coalesce in the present by way of retentions and protentions, the latter temporal dimensions translating at an experiential level into remembrances and expectations (Husserl 1964, 1970, 1973, 1977, 1980, 1981, 1989). It is of interest to note with respect to internal time consciousness that philosopher Dan Lloyd showed how Husserl's phenomenological analyses of time based on experience are sustained by fMRI images of the brain. Lloyd in fact won an award from a scientific institute for his work (see Bower 2002 and Sheets-Johnstone 2004). His intricate studies show that the whole brain is involved in the performance of tasks and that time in the Husserlian sense of internal time consciousness is central to conscious activity.

Waiting can bring us face to face with the temporality of our aliveness, with our "zero-point of orientation," with the "hereness" of our being, with the meanings and values of our immediate surrounding world, and with the temporal nature of consciousness itself.

Paradoxically enough, it is in and through our awareness of the impermanence of movement—movement inside and out—that we have the possibility not only of enduring the experience of time on our hands but of settling comfortably and inquisitively into the experience of waiting. In doing so, we are not trying to kill time, as Heidegger intimates in his walking back and forth or drawing figures in the sand. We are living in the fleeting yet qualitatively remarkable temporal dynamics of movement, experiencing its evenness and unevenness, its hesitations, accents, pauses—even in the process of walking back and forth or drawing figures in the sand.

Ponderabilia 13:

THINKING IN MOVEMENT

Stephen Jay Gould, longtime contributor to *Natural History* magazine and highly revered evolutionary biologist, extols the extraordinary significance of movement to learning in an article titled "Evolution by Walking" (Gould 1995). He begins exemplifying the significance by singling out "the great dramatic conflicts between women and sinister forces—Fay Wray and King Kong, Sigourney Weaver and the "Aliens," and so on. But, as he puts it, "I still cast my vote, in this genre, for Raquel Welch and the antibodies in Fantastic Voyage." His reason: The conflict between Welch and the antibodies illustrates a concept by way of moving bodies. In particular, by scaling the body up or down, "the visceral" is used "to grasp the cerebral." On the basis of his own experience, he adds, "I have, for example, been a pawn (literally) in a very large game of chess—and I really did understand the game better after I moved doggedly forward, slipped cleverly on a diagonal to murder a brother of another color, and finally succumbed to the ecclesiastical sweep of a distant bishop along the same diagonal." He notes too that "museum exhibits on the heart may treat each visitor as a blood cell moving through corridors shaped as vena cava and aorta, into rooms modeled as auricles and ventricles" (ibid., p. 10). In short, through his examples and discussions, he shows that movement and conceptualization are pedagogically of moment, that one can indeed effectively use "the visceral to grasp the cerebral."

At the end of the article, he looks back to Aristotle and his peripatetic followers who walked their way into knowledge. They did not sit at desks nor were they ensconced in ivory towers. On the contrary, they "valued the linkage of cogitation and ambulation" (ibid., p. 15).

The evolutionary point Gould makes has to do with what we may well call "wandering," that is, drawing lines that don't proceed in straight-line linear fashion. What Gould wants to demonstrate in living terms is the impropriety of conceiving evolution as a linear phenomenon leading to humans at the top rather than as a branching history that mirrors the temporal order in which species actually evolved. A museum organized along just such branching lines, Gould says, involves visitors "viscerally by walking rather than only conceptually by reading" (ibid., p. 13).

The linkage between thinking and movement is complex (Sheets-Johnstone 1981, 1999/2011, 2009). What Gould identifies as "the visceral" is basically kinesthetic experience, a qualitatively structured dynamic experience in its own right, but one that is affectively qualified, precisely as in Gould's description of moving "doggedly forward," and "slipping cleverly on a diagonal." Clearly, such kinesthetic/affective realities are cognitively inflected. It is not only in a game of chess that one thinks in movement. Thinking is modeled on the body; the body is a semantic template (Sheets-Johnstone 1990). We might ask, for example, how did stone tools originate? Where did the idea come from?

174

Over and over again, anthropologists claim that stone tools replaced teeth but go no further in their explanation (see Sheets-Johnstone 1990 for a thorough review and analysis). Systematic reflection and research on the topic, however, shows that corporeal concepts grounded the invention of stone tools. Teeth bite through flesh and vegetable matter; they grind through sinewy material; they scrape or strip off surface layers of objects. They are multi-purpose tools for transforming an original material into something softer, smaller, and juicier. The transformation is a tactile-kinesthetic phenomenon.

Moreover if one examines one's teeth themselves in relation to early stone tool-making, one readily grasps a further relationship between the "visceral and the cerebral." Molars are complexly grooved objects. Declivities and ridges are not symmetrically aligned. The occlusal—biting—surfaces of molars are palpably uneven and thickly rather than pointedly edged. In contrast, incisors are rather simple tactile objects. They have a single, even, lingually traceable edge. They are thin rather than thick and their slightly rounded labial surface is smooth and even; their lingual surface, though palpably curved, is otherwise uncomplicated and smooth rather than irregular. In brief, if one examines one's teeth, one finds palpable differences between molars and incisors. Just so, if one examines early stone tool-making, one finds palpable differences between a core tool and a flake tool.

That thinking is modeled on the body is apparent not only from deepened understandings of how stone tools replaced teeth, but from deepened understanding of counting, of drawing, of language, and even of the concept of death (Sheets-Johnstone 1990). Claims, stories, or theories about how counting originated, for example, commonly take numbers for granted. Yet it is clear from studies of non-Western cultures that counting is a matter of noticing similarities, and of matching by comparing. How then, we may ask, did ancestral hominids come to an awareness of "how many" without giving a number to each in turn? And how did giving a number to each in turn originate?

When we recognize the body as a semantic template, answers to these questions become apparent on the basis of experience. Two striding legs, two swinging arms, inhaling and exhaling, a front and a back, and so on, all are—and were—originally felt as qualitatively matched correspondences, that is, as binary phenomena. How these experiences ultimately evolved into numerical counting becomes evident precisely by way of recognizing that in certain human societies, counting takes place only on and with the tactile-kinesthetic body, or, in other words, that counting cannot proceed without the person actually touching the body part signifying the intended number. In one such system—complex, to be sure—the person commences with the little finger of the left hand and proceeds from there to the other fingers on that hand, to the thumb, the wrist, the elbow joint, the shoulder, and so on, the series ending with the little finger of the right hand (Levy-Bruhl 1966, p. 163; Sheets-Johnstone 1990).

Claims, stories, and theories about how a verbal language originated similarly take for granted basic bodily experiences that ground the very possibility of a verbal language. To begin with, the possibility of verbal language lies in the tactility of the tongue. In the beginning, as psychologist Jean Piaget's studies show, the tongue is preeminently an organ of touch rather than of taste. The tongue discovers the hardness or softness, the jaggedness or smoothness, the flatness or roundedness, the warmth or coolness, and the dryness or moistness of objects. An infant's beginning play with sounds in the first year of life is testimonial to its primordial communion with the world by way of touch. Indeed, an infant discovers itself as a sound-maker, and in turn discovers tactile-kinesthetic invariants in sound-making. Just such awarenesses were requisite at the dawn of verbal language. The sound emitted in pressing the lips together, for example, is altogether different from the sound emitted in bringing lips together and puffing air out as one opens them: the tactile-kinesthetic difference between the sound "m" and the sound "p" is immediately apparent. The discovery of just such tactile-kinesthetic invariants are mandatory to the invention of a common verbal language (Sheets-Johnstone 1990).

In sum, thinking in movement is a basic animate capacity, a built-in of all animate life. A gibbon ape brachiating its way through the middle storey of a rain forest is surely thinking in movement. So also is a worm. Darwin concluded from his extended and detailed studies that "worms, although standing low in the scale of organization, possess some degree of intelligence." He added, "This will strike every one as very improbable; but it may be doubted whether we know enough about the nervous system of the lower animals to justify our natural distrust of such a conclusion. With respect to the small size of the cerebral ganglia, we should remember what a mass of inherited knowledge, with some power of adapting means to an end, is crowded into the minute brain of a worker ant" (Darwin 1976 [1881], p. 58).

When we stop to think about thinking, we begin to realize the debt we owe to our tactile-kinesthetic bodies. Gould notes the "fundamental change that made human evolution possible: upright posture and bipedal locomotion" (Gould 1995, p. 15). We can elaborate his observation in the following meaningful ways. A dynamically attuned body that knows the world and makes its way within it kinetically is thoughtfully attuned to its own body and to the variable qualia of both its own movement and the movement of things in its surrounding world—to forceful, swift, slow, straight, swerving, flaccid, tense, sudden, up, down, and much more. Fundamental concepts derive from the tactile-kinesthetic body, its tactile-kinesthetic invariants and its vital, living experiences of movement. Movement and thinking go hand in hand. As I elsewhere commented, "Caught up in an adult world, we easily lose sight of movement and of our fundamental capacity to think in movement. Any time we care to turn our attention to it, however, there it is" (Sheets-Johnstone 1981, 1999/2011, 2009).

Ponderabilia 14:

ON UNSTEADY SOULS, THE FLEETINGNESS OF MOVEMENT, AND THE IMAGINATIVE CONSCIOUSNESS OF MOVEMENT

Oddly enough, "unsteady souls" are firmly rooted in their bodies. They are not whirling about in a vortex of "doings," but are alive to the dynamics of their own movement. In effect, they have not left their bodies behind and unattended, and they do not treat them as mere instruments. Being attuned to the ongoing dynamics of their own animation, however, does not mean they are consumed in a self-centered universe. On the contrary, they are engaged in the movement of life all about them, in the full-bodied realities that make up their surrounding lifeworld as well as in their own full-bodied realities. They are thus corps engagés, enmeshed in whatever the immediate situation, with a sense of its flow, its intensity, its constrictedness, its expansiveness, and so on. Feeling alive is precisely for unsteady souls because unsteady souls are unfalteringly sturdy enough to live in the fleeting, inherently changing nature and realities of life itself and the animation and dynamics that define their aliveness.

Linear design and linear pattern are both spatial dimensions of movement, as we have seen, but they are notably more complex than we might think. The linear design of a moving body—or a body at rest—is directly perceived by others. With respect to self-movement, however, the design is an imaginative construction. While we can visually perceive an extended forward-reaching arm of our own or that of someone else as forming a straight line, we imaginatively constitute the vertical line we ourselves form in standing and the twisted linear design we create in turning our head and upper torso to look at something behind us. In short, when it is a question of our own movement, we not uncommonly have an imaginative consciousness of the linear designs of our moving bodies. Indeed, we are virtually always on the inside of our own movement. We are kinesthetically, not visually, aware of our moving bodies.

Our imaginative consciousness of movement is actually rooted in fleeting tactilities as well as movement. When we flex an arm or a leg, we feel not only muscular pulls and the closing of a joint, but, as noted earlier, the progressive coming together of two bodily surfaces: forearm and upper arm touch at the inside of the elbow joint; calf and back of thigh touch at the inside of the knee joint. Such tactilely-informed kinesthetic awarenesses are part and parcel of our imaginative consciousness of movement, part and parcel of those imagined bodily lines our bodies dynamically form in the process of moving.

We might note that what is commonly taken for granted as an everyday fact of life, something people simply assume in the form "postures" and "postural awareness," is a complex phenomenon warranting examination. Barring mirrors and third-person perspectives, our postures and postural awarenesses are not basically visual but kinesthetic, and not basically perceptual but imaginative phenomena dependent on the felt realities of kinesthesia. To come to this realization requires careful examinations of experience and perhaps even training in bodily awareness, something akin to what neuropsychologist Edmund Jacobson called "auto-sensory observation" (Jacobson 1929, 1967, 1970) and to what phenomenologists call "bracketing" (Husserl 1989, p. 27; Sheets-Johnstone 1999/2011, pp. 188-90/pp. 163-64). What we commonly take for granted, in other words, is not uncommonly something so much a part of our everyday lives that we fail to take notice of it and thereby pass over any genuine experiences and understandings of it. In becoming aware of the linear design of our bodies at any moment or over any particular span of time, we are indeed actually synthesizing separately felt joint angularities.

Those separately felt joint angularities, products of muscular tensions, support the imagined lines we draw but do not tell the whole story. In finer terms, while the angle of any joint is perceived kinesthetically, the distance between joints cannot be perceived; it can only be imagined, and imagined kinetically in the form of a drawn line. Similarly, muscular contractions can be perceived in the form of bodily tensions, but they too are localized. In short, there is no continuous set of receptors by which we can follow the skeletal outline of our body either at rest or as it moves. That outline may be followed only by an imaginative consciousness in the form of a line or constellation of lines.

Linear patterns created by movement are similarly not perceived or perceivable but are through and through imaginatively constituted phenomena. The patterns emerge in the form of imagined trajectories that a moving body draws in the process of moving. Indeed, whenever we move, we draw imaginary lines with various parts of our bodies and our bodies as a whole, as in reaching for a book on a shelf above us, sweeping up the shards left by a broken glass, running down the street, or turning a corner. What is imaginatively constituted in all instances are lines.

Lines are clearly spatial entities, whether actually drawn on paper and perceived or whether imaginatively constituted and followed. When imaginatively brought to life, however, that is, when experienced as a linear design or pattern created by movement, they are not purely and solely spatial entities. When we apprehend any moving body—our own or that of another person—as creating a linear design and pattern, whether in stirring a cake batter, hammering a nail, kicking a ball, or zigzagging to avoid colliding with someone, we temporalize a spatial dimension of movement in the course of imaginatively spatializing the directional line or lines themselves. In other words, being essentially kinetic spatial phenomena, the lines created by moving bodies are inherently temporal in character.

We can bring that inherent temporal character to self-evidence in a focal and even striking way by drawing figure eights in the air—or scallops or spirals or the number three or the letter "m," for example. In so doing, we experience the imaginatively drawn line as a temporal as well as spatial phenomenon, a temporal phenomenon not simply in terms of its duration, but in terms of its pauses, quicknesses, attenuations, and so on. Indeed, lines have an intricate dynamic structure.

It is hardly surprising, then, that the lines we draw, whether imaginative or real, have affective overtones and are not in fact uncommonly inspired, that is, motivated by our affective lives. We might feel rushed in getting to a meeting, for example, lethargic in getting out of bed, an ebullient energy in approaching a friend, a seething anger in writing a letter, a hesitancy in touching a jellyfish, an excited curiosity in exploring a cave, and so on. In each instance, the linear designs of our bodies and the linear patterns we draw are suffused with what infant psychiatrist and clinical psychologist Daniel Stern aptly terms "vitality affects" such as "surging," "explosive," "drawn out," "fleeting," and so on (Stern 1985, pp. 53-61).

An attentiveness to the bodily lines we create and the linear patterns we draw in moving can in fact readily call our attention to the impermanence of movement. To experience the impermanence of movement as of life itself puts us at the heart of Nature and of our own natural history as *Homo sapiens sapiens*, a particular species of morphologies-in-motion that moves bipedally. Our imaginative consciousness of movement figuratively ties our life together as it ties our footsteps together. We cannot go backward, only forward; we can retrace our steps, but only in the form of a new line.

The Spanish poet Antonio Machado wrote eloquently of the foundational impermanence of life and the movement that grounds it (Machado 1982). He describes us as "wayfarers" or "wanderers" whose path is underdetermined: the source of our path is unknown or not remembered and has no goal. Indeed, our paths themselves wander. What humans do to make up for the impermanence of their movement through life and of their lives as a whole is draw figuratively on their imaginative consciousness of movement. We humans indeed dynamically recreate the lines along which we have travelled, the paths that our lives once followed; and we dynamically create the paths along which we are now moving and might move in the future, the path of the moment and the paths along which life might take us. We temporalize by way of movement. We make connections, we wander, creating linear patterns as we go, patterns that are always qualitatively distinct in virtue of the qualitative dynamic realities of movement itself.

Writing in a different context but resonating fully with Machado's verse, social anthropologist Tim Ingold insightfully observes, life "threads its way through the world"; "what matters is not the final destination, but all the interesting things that occur along the way. For wherever you are, there is somewhere further you can go" (Ingold 2007, pp. 103, 170).

Ponderabilia References

Ponderabilia 1: On Movement and Feeling Alive

Cunningham, Merce. 1968. *Notes on Choreography*, ed. Frances Starr. New York: Something Else Press.

Jantzen, Kelly J., Fred L. Steinberg, and J. A. Scott Kelso. 2008. "Coordination Dynamics of Large-scale Neural Circuitry Underlying Rhythmic Sensorimotor Behavior." *Journal of Cognitive Neuroscience* 21, no. 12: 2420-2433.

Kelso, J. A. Scott. 1995. *Dynamic Patterns: The Self-Organization of Brain and Behavior*. Cambridge, MA: Bradford Books/MIT Press.

Kelso, J. A. Scott and David A. Engstrom. 2006. *The Complementary Nature*. Cambridge, MA: Bradford Books/MIT Press.

Lawrence, D. H. 1932. *Apocalypse*. New York: Viking Press.

Oullier, Olivier and J. A. Scott Kelso. 2009. "Social Coordination from the Perspective of Coordination Dynamics." In *Encyclopedia of Complexity and Systems Sciences*, ed. R. A. Meyers. Berlin: Springer-Verlag, pp. 8198-8212.

Sheets-Johnstone, Maxine. 1999/expanded 2nd ed. 2011. *The Primacy of Movement*, vol. 14 Advances in Consciousness Research. Amsterdam/Philadelphia: John Benjamins Publishing.

Spitz, René A. 1983. *Dialogues from Infancy*, ed. Robert N. Emde. New York: International Universities Press.

Stern, Daniel N. 1985. *The Interpersonal World of the Infant: A View from Psychoanalysis and Developmental Psychology*. New York: Basic Books.

Ponderabilia 2: It's Amazing!

Crick, Francis and Christof Koch. 1992. "The Problem of Consciousness." *Scientific American* 267(3): 153-159.

Calvin, William. 1987. "The Brain as a Darwin Machine." *Nature* 330: 33-34.

Furuhjelm, Mirjam, Axel Ingelman-Sundbert, and Claes Wirsén. 1976. *A Child Is Born*, rev. ed. New York: Delacourte Press.

Freedberg, David and Vittorio Gallese. 2007. "Motion, Emotion and Empathy in Esthetic Experience." *Trends in Cognitive Science*, 11(5), 197–203.

Gallagher, Shaun. 2000 (December). "Phenomenological and Experimental Research on Embodied Experience." Paper presented at *Atelier phénomenologie et cognition, Phénomenologie et Cognition Research Group*, CREA, Paris.

Gibbs, Raymond W. Jr. 2006. *Embodiment and Cognitive Science*. New York: Cambridge University Press.

Harding, Robert S. O. 1975. "Meat-Eating and Hunting in Baboons." In *Socioecology and Psychology of Primates*, ed. Russell H. Tuttle. The Hague: Mouton Publishers, pp. 245-257.

Lakoff, George and Mark Johnson. 1999. *Philosophy in the Flesh*. Chicago: University of Chicago Press.

Raloff, Janet. 1996 (November 30). "How the Brain Knows When to Stop Eating." *Science News*, pp. 341-343.

Robeck, Mildred C. 1978. *Infants and Children*. New York: McGraw-Hill Book Co.

Sheets-Johnstone, Maxine. 1994. *The Roots of Power: Animate Form and Gendered Bodies*. Chicago: Open Court Publishing.

Sheets-Johnstone, Maxine. 1999a. "Emotions and Movement: A Beginning Empirical-Phenomenological Analysis of Their Relationship." *Journal of Consciousness Studies*, vol. 6, No. 11-12: 259-277.

Sheets-Johnstone, Maxine. 1999b/expanded 2nd ed. 2011. *The Primacy of Movement*, vol. 14 Advances in Consciousness Research Series. Amsterdam/Philadelphia: John Benjamins Publishing.

Sheets-Johnstone, Maxine. 2008. *The Roots of Morality*. University Park, PA: Pennsylvania State University Press.

Thompson, Evan. 2007. *Mind in Life: Biology, Phenomenology, and the Sciences of Mind*. Cambridge, MA: Belknap Press of Harvard University Press.

Varela, Francisco J. and Natalie Depraz. 2005. "At the Source of Time: Valence and the Constitutional Dynamics of Affect." *Journal of Consciousness Studies* vol. 12, No. 8-10. (Special issue on "Emotion Experience," ed. Giovanna Colombetti and Evan Thompson), pp. 61-81.

Varela, Francisco J., Evan Thompson, and Eleanor Rosch. 1991. *The Embodied Mind*. Cambridge, MA: MIT Press.

Windle, William F. 1971. *Physiology of the Fetus*. Springfield, IL: Charles C. Thomas.

Zeki, Semir. 1992. "The Visual Image in Mind and Brain." *Scientific American* 267(3): 69-76.

Ponderabilia 3: On Behavior and Movement

Gleitman, Henry. *Psychology* 1981. New York: W. W. Norton & Co.

Muller, Herbert. 1943. *Science and Criticism*. New Haven. Yale University Press.

Skinner, B. F. 1964. "Behaviorism at Fifty." In *Behaviorism and Phenomenology: Contrasting Bases for Modern Psychology*, ed. T. W. Wann. Chicago: University of Chicago Press.

Skinner, B. F. 1974. *About Behaviorism*. New York: Knopf.

Sheets-Johnstone, Maxine. 1999/expanded 2nd ed. 2011. *The Primacy of Movement*, vol. 14 Advances in Consciousness Research Series. Amsterdam/Philadelphia: John Benjamins Publishing.

Watson, John B. 1939. *Behaviorism*, 2nd ed. Chicago: University of Chicago Press.

Watson, Robert I. 1979. "Skinner on Work as a Scientist, Operant Conditioning, and Freedom and Control." In *Basic Writings in the History of Psychology*, ed. R. I. Watson. New York: Oxford University Press.

Ponderabilia 4: Pulsing With Life!

All references to Aristotle are to sections marked in the margins of any translation of his work. I have used *The Complete Works of Aristotle*, 2 volumes, rev. Oxford translation, ed. Jonathan Barnes (Bollingen Series LXXI.2). Princeton: Princeton University Press.

Curtis, Helena. 1975. *Biology*, 2nd ed. New York: Worth Publishers.

Ponderabilia 5: How Common Misunderstandings of Movement Occlude Its Qualitative Realities

Descartes, René. 1985 [1644]. *The Philosophical Writings of Descartes*, vol. 1, trans. John Cottingham, Robert Stoothoff, and Dugald Murdoch. Cambridge: Cambridge University Press.

Sheets-Johnstone, Maxine. 1966. *The Phenomenology of Dance*. Madison: University of Wisconsin; second editions: London: Dance Books Ltd. 1979; New York: Arno Press, 1980.

Sheets-Johnstone, Maxine. 1979. "On Movement and Objects in Motion: The Phenomenology of the Visible in Dance." *Journal of Aesthetic Education* vol. 13, no. 2: 33-46.

Sheets-Johnstone, Maxine. 1998. "Consciousness: A Natural History." *Journal of Consciousness Studies*, vol. 5, no. 3: 260-294.

Sheets-Johnstone, Maxine. 1999/expanded 2nd ed. 2011. *The Primacy of Movement*, vol. 14, Advances in Consciousness Research. Amsterdam/Philadelphia: John Benjamins Publishing.

Sheets-Johnstone, Maxine. 2009. *The Corporeal Turn: An Interdisciplinary Reader*. Exeter, United Kingdom: Imprint Academic.

Sheets-Johnstone, Maxine. 2009. "Kinesthetic Experience: Understanding Movement Inside and Out." *Body, Movement And Dance In Psychotherapy* 5, No. 2: 111-127.

Ponderabilia 6: Kinesthetic Memory

Husserl, Edmund. 1970. *The Crisis of European Sciences and Transcendental Phenomenology*, trans. David Carr. Evanston, IL: Northwestern University Press.

Husserl, Edmund. 1973. *Cartesian Meditations*, trans. Dorion Cairns. The Hague: Martinus Nijhoff.

Husserl, Edmund. 1980. *Ideas Pertaining to a Pure Phenomenology and to a Phenomenological Philosophpy: Book 3 (Ideas III)*, trans. Ted E. Klein and William E. Pohl. The Hague: Martinus Nijhoff.

Husserl, Edmund. 1989. *Ideas Pertaining to a Pure Phenomenology and to a Phenomenological Philosophy: Book 2 (Ideas II)*, trans. R. Rojcewicz and A. Schuwer. Boston: Kluwer Academic Publishers.

Luria, Alexander R. 1966. *Human Brain and Psychological Processes*, trans. Basil Haigh. New York: Harper & Row.

Luria, Alexander R. 1973. *The Working Brain*, trans. Basil Haigh. Harmondsworth, Middlesex, England: Penguin Books.

Luria, Alexander R. 1980. *Higher Cortical Functions in Man*, 2nd ed., trans. Basil Haigh. New York: Basic Books.

Heidegger, Martin. 1962. *Being and Time*, trans. John Macquarrie and Edward Robinson. New York: Harper & Row.

Searle, John. 1992. *The Rediscovery of Mind*. Cambridge, MA: Bradford Books/MIT Press.

Sheets-Johnstone, Maxine. 1999/expanded 2nd ed. 2011. *The Primacy of Movement*, vol. 14, Advances in Consciousness Research. Amsterdam/Philadelphia: John Benjamins Publishing.

Sheets-Johnstone, Maxine. 2003. "Kinesthetic Memory." *Theoria et Historia Scientiarum* (Nicolas Copernicus University) VII/I (Special issue on Phenomenology and Cognitive Science, ed. Shaun Gallagher and Natalie Depraz): 69-92.

Sheets-Johnstone, Maxine. 2012. "Kinesthetic Memory: Further Critical Reflections and Constructive Analyses." In *Body Memory*, ed. Sabine Koch, Thomas Fuchs, Michela Summa and Cornelia Müller. Amsterdam/Philadelphia: John Benjamins pp. 43-72

Ponderabilia 7: The Gift of Play

Brown, Stuart. 1994 (December). "Animal Play." *National Geographic.*

Brown, Stuart. 1998. "Play as an Organizing Principle: Clinical Evidence and Personal Observation." In *Animal Play: Evolutionary, Comparative, and Ecological Perspectives*, ed. Marc Bekoff and John A. Byers. Cambridge: Cambridge University Press, pp. 243-259.

Darwin, Charles. 1965 [1872]. *The Expression of the Emotions in Man and Animals.* Chicago: University of Chicago Press.

Ingold, Tim and Jo Lee Vergunst. 2008. "Introduction." In *Ways of Walking: Ethnography and Practice on Foot*, ed. Tim Ingold and Jo Lee Vergunst. Hampshire, UK/Burlington, VT: Ashgate Publishing, pp. 1-19.

Joyce, James. 1947. "A Painful Case." In *The Portable James Joyce*. New York: Viking Press, pp. 118-129.

Sheets-Johnstone, Maxine. 1986. "Existential Fit and Evolutionary Continuities." *Synthese* 66: 219-248.

Sheets-Johnstone, Maxine. 2003. "Child's Play: A Multidisciplinary Perspective." *Human Studies* 26: 409-430.

Sheets-Johnstone, Maxine. 2008. *The Roots of Morality*. University Park, PA: Pennsylvania State University Press.

Sheets-Johnstone, Maxine. 2009. *The Corporeal Turn: An Interdisciplinary Reader.* Exeter, United Kingdom: Imprint Academic..

Van Hooff, J. A. R. A. M. 1969. "The Facial Displays of the Catarrhine Monkeys and Apes." In *Primate Ethology*, ed. Desmond Morris. Garden City, NY: Anchor Books, pp. 9-88.

Van Hooff, J. A. R. A. M. 1972. "A Comparative Approach to the Phylogeny of Laughter and Smiling." In *Non-Verbal Communication*, ed. R. A. Hinde. Cambridge, MA: Cambridge University Press, pp. 209-241.

Ponderabilia 8: On Creativity, Wonder, and the Unsung Kinetic Imagination

Da Vinci, Leonardo. 1959. *Philosophical Diary*, trans. Wade Baskin. New York: Wisdom Library.

Fink, Eugen. 1981. "The Problem of the Phenomenology of Edmund Husserl," trans. Robert M. Harlan. In *Apriori and World: European Contributions to Husserlian Phenomenology*, ed. William McKenna, Robert M. Harlan, and Laurence E. Winters. The Hague: Martinus Nijhoff, pp. 21-55.

Jung, Carl G. 1976. *Psychological Types*, trans. R. F. C. Hull. Bollingen Series XX. Princeton: Princeton University Press.

Sheets-Johnstone, Maxine. 1966. *The Phenomenology of Dance*. Madison: University of Wisconsin Press; second editions: London: Dance Books Ltd., 1979; New York: Arno Press, 1980.

Sheets-Johnstone, Maxine. 1999. "Emotions and Movement: A Beginning Empirical-Phenomenological Analysis of Their Relationship. *Journal of Consciousness Studies* 6, No. 11-12: 259-277.

Sheets-Johnstone, Maxine. 2006. *"Sur la nature de la confiance."* In *Les Moments de la Confiance*, ed. Albert Ogien and Louis Quéré. Paris: Economica.

Sheets-Johnstone, Maxine. 2008. *The Roots of Morality*. University Park, PA: Pennsylvania State University Press.

Tomasello, Michael and Josep Call. 1997. *Primate Cognition*. New York: Oxford University Press.

Ponderabilia 9: Thoughts About Space, Motors—and More!

Aristotle: All references to Aristotle are to sections marked in the margins of any translation of his work. I have used *The Complete Works of Aristotle*, 2 volumes, rev. Oxford translation, ed. Jonathan Barnes (Bollingen Series LXXI.2). Princeton: Princeton University Press.

Bernstein, Nicolas. 1984. *Human Motor Actions: Bernstein Reassessed*, ed. H. T. A. Whiting. New York: Elsevier Publishing Co.

Darwin, Charles. 1987 [1838]. *Charles Darwin's Notebooks, 1836-1844*, ed. Paul H. Barrett, Peter J. Gautrey, Sandra Herbert, David Kohn, Sydney Smith. Ithaca: Cornell University Press.

Dennett, Daniel. 1991. *Consciousness Explained*. Boston: Little, Brown and Company.

Gowitzke, Barbara A. and Morris Milner. 1988. *Scientific Bases of Human Movement*, 3rd ed. Baltimore: Williams and Wilkins.

Sheets-Johnstone, Maxine. 2003. "Kinesthetic Memory." *Theoria et Historia Scientiarum* (Nicolas Copernicus University) vol. 7, no. 1: 69-92.

Sheets-Johnstone, Maxine. 2009a. "Animation: The Fundamental, Essential, and Properly Descriptive Concept." *Continental Philosophy Review* 42: 375-400.

Sheets-Johnstone, Maxine. 2009b. *The Corporeal Turn: An Interdisciplinary Reader*. Exeter, United Kingdom: Imprint Academic.

Sheets-Johnstone, Maxine. 2012. "Fundamental and Inherently Interrelated Aspects of Animation." In *Moving Ourselves, Moving Others: Motion and Emotion in Intersubjectivity, Consciousness and Language*, ed. Ad Foolen, Ulrike Lüdtke, Jordan Zlatev, Tim Racine. Amsterdam/Philadelphia: John Benjamins Publishing, pp. 29-55.

Umtilà, Carlos. 2007. "Consciousness and Control of Action." In *The Cambridge Handbook of Consciousness*, ed. Philip D. Zelazo, Morris Moscovitch, and Evan Thompson. Cambridge: Cambridge University Press, pp. 327-351.

Ponderabilia 10: In the Beginning . . .

Bruner, Jerome. 1990. *Acts of Meaning*. Cambridge, MA: Harvard University Press.

Husserl, Edmund. 1989. *Ideas Pertaining to a Pure Phenomenology and to a Phenomenological Philosophy: Book 2 (Ideas II)*, trans. R. Rojcewicz and A. Schuwer. Boston: Kluwer Academic Publishers.

Laverack, M. S. 1976. "External Proprioceptors." In *Structure and Function of Proprioceptors in the Invertebrates*, ed. P. J. Mill. London: Chapman and Hall, pp. 1-63.

Lissman, H. W. 1950. "Proprioceptors." *Physiological Mechanisms in Animal Behavior* (Symposia of the Society for Experimental Biology), vol. 4. New York: Academic Press, pp. 34-59.

Sheets-Johnstone, Maxine. 1990. *The Roots of Thinking*. Philadelphia: Temple University Press.

Sheets-Johnstone, Maxine. 1998. "Consciousness: A Natural History." *Journal of Consciousness Studies* vol. 5, no.3: 260-294.

Sheets-Johnstone, Maxine. 1999/expanded 2nd ed. 2011. *The Primacy of Movement*, vol. 14, Advances in Consciousness Research. Amsterdam/Philadelphia: John Benjamins Publishing.

Sheets-Johnstone, Maxine. 2008. "Getting to the Heart of Emotions and Consciousness." In *Handbook of Cognitive Science*, ed. Paco Calvo and Antonio Gomila. Amsterdam/Boston: Elsevier Publishers.

Sheets-Johnstone, Maxine. 2009. "Animation: The Fundamental, Essential, and Properly Descriptive Concept." *Continental Philosophy Review* 42: 375-400.

Sheets-Johnstone, Maxine. 2012. "Fundamental and Inherently Interrelated Aspects of Animation." In *Moving Ourselves, Moving Others: Motion and Emotion in Intersubjectivity, Consciousness and Language*, ed. Ad Foolen Ulrike Lüdtke, Jordan Zlatev, Tim Racine. Amsterdam/Philadelphia: John Benjamins Publishing, pp. 29-55.

Stern, Daniel N. 1985. *The Interpersonal World of the Infant: A View from Psychoanalysis and Developmental Psychology*. New York: Basic Books.

Ponderabilia 11: Synergies of Meaningful Movement

Sheets-Johnstone, Maxine. 1990. *The Roots of Thinking*. Philadelphia: Temple University Press.

Sheets-Johnstone, Maxine. 1994. *The Roots of Power: Animate Form and Gendered Bodies*. Chicago: University of Chicago Press.

Sheets-Johnstone, Maxine. 1999. "Sensory-Kinetic Understandings of Language." *Evolution of Communication* vol. 3, no. 2: 149-183.

Sheets-Johnstone, Maxine. 2004. "On Bacteria, Corporeal Representation, Neandertals, and Martha Graham." In *In the Beginning: Origins of Semiosis*, ed. Morana Alac and Patrizia Violi. Bologna, Italy: Brepols Turnhout, pp. 105-136. Included as Chapter XI in Sheets-Johnstone 2009, *The Corporeal Turn: An Interdisciplinary Reader*. Exeter, United Kingdom: Imprint Academic.

Sheets-Johnstone, Maxine. 2006. "Essential Clarifications of 'Self-Affection' and Husserl's 'Sphere of Ownness': First Steps toward a Pure Phenomenology of (Human) Nature." *Continental Philosophy Review* 39: 361-391.

Sheets-Johnstone, Maxine. 2008. "Getting to the Heart of Emotions and Consciousness." In *Handbook of Cognitive Science*, ed. Paco Calvo and Antonio Gomila. Amsterdam/Boston: Elsevier, pp. 453-465.

Sheets-Johnstone, Maxine. 2009a. *The Roots of Morality*. University Park, PA: Pennsylvania State University Press.

Sheets-Johnstone, Maxine. 2009b. "Animation: The Fundamental, Properly Descriptive, and Essential Concept." *Continental Philosophy Review* 42: 375-400.

Ponderabilia 12: On the Temporality of Our Aliveness

Bower, Bruce. 2002. "Spreading Consciousness." *Science News* 162 (16): 251-252.

Heidegger, Martin. 1995. *The Fundamental Concepts of Metaphysics: World, Finitude, Solitude*, trans. William McNeill and Nicholas Walker. Bloomington: Indiana University Press.

Husserl, Edmund. 1964. *The Phenomenology of Internal Time Consciousness*, trans. James S. Churchill, ed. M. Heidegger. Bloomington: Indiana University Press.

Husserl, Edmund. 1970. "The Origin of Geometry." In *The Crisis of European Sciences and Transcendental Phenomenology*, trans. David Carr. Evanston, IL: Northwestern University Press, pp. 353-378.

Husserl, Edmund. 1973. *Cartesian Meditations*, trans. Dorion Cairns. The Hague: Martinus Nijhoff.

Husserl, Edmund. 1977. *Phenomenological Psychology*, trans. John Scanlon. The Hague: Martinus Nijhoff.

Husserl, Edmund. 1980. *Ideas Pertaining to a Pure Phenomenology and to a Phenomenological Philosophy: Book 3 (Ideas III)*, trans. Ted E. Klein and William E. Pohl. The Hague: Martinus Nijhoff.

Husserl, Edmund. 1981. "The World of the Living Present and the Constitution of the Surrounding World External to the Organism," trans. Frederick a. Elliston and Lenore Langsdorf. In *Husserl: Shorter Works*, ed. Peter McCormick and Frederick Elliston. Notre Dame: University of Notre Dame Press., pp. 238-250.

Husserl, Edmund. 1989. *Ideas Pertaining to a Pure Phenomenology and to a Phenomenological Philosophy, Book 2 (Ideas II)*, trans. R. Rojcewicz and A. Schuwer. Boston: Kluwer Academic Publishers.

Sartre, Jean-Paul. 1956. *Being and Nothingness*, trans. Hazel E. Barnes. New York: Philosophical Library.

Sheets-Johnstone, Maxine. 1999. "Emotions and Movement: A Beginning Empirical-Phenomenological Analysis of Their Relationship." *Journal of Consciousness Studies*, vol. 6, no. 11-12: 259-277. Included as Chapter VIII in Sheets-Johnstone, Maxine 2009.

Sheets-Johnstone, Maxine. 2004. "Preserving Integrity Against Colonization." *Phenomenology and the Cognitive Sciences* 3: 240-261.

Sheets-Johnstone, Maxine. 2008. *The Roots of Morality*. University Park, PA: Pennsylvania State University Press.

Sheets-Johnstone, Maxine. 2009. *The Corporeal Turn: An Interdisciplinary Reader*. Exeter, United Kingdom: Imprint Academic.

Ponderabilia 13: Thinking in Movement

Darwin, Charles. 1976 [1881]. *The Formation of Vegetable Mould Through the Action of Worms with Observations on Their Habits*. Ontario, CA: Bookworm Publishing Co.

Gould, Stephen Jay. 1995. "Evolution by Walking." *Natural History*, vol. 104, no. 3: 10-15.

Levy-Bruhl, Lucien. 1966. *How Natives Think*, trans. Lilian A. Clare. New York: Washington Square Press.

Sheets-Johnstone, Maxine. 1981. "Thinking in Movement." *Journal of Aesthetics and Art Criticism*, vol. 39, no. 4: 399-407.

Sheets-Johnstone, Maxine. 1990. *The Roots of Thinking*. Philadelphia: Temple University Press.

Sheets-Johnstone, Maxine. 1999/2011 and 2009. "Thinking in Movement." Sizably expanded version of 1981 article in *The Primacy of Movement*, Chapter 12, and in *The Corporeal Turn*, Chapter 2.

Ponderabilia 14: On Unsteady Souls, the Fleetingness of Movement, and the Imaginative Consciousness of Movement

Husserl, Edmund. 1989. *Ideas Pertaining to a Pure Phenomenology and to a Phenomenological Philosophy, Book 2 (Ideas II)*, trans. R. Rojcewicz and A. Schuwer. Dordrecht: Kluwer Academic Publishers.

Ingold, Tim. 2007. *Lines: A Brief History*. London/New York: Routledge.

Jacobson, Edmund. 1929. *Progressive Relaxation*. Chicago: University of Chicago Press.

Jacobson, Edmund. 1967. *Biology of Emotions*. Springfield, IL: Charles C. Thomas.

Jacobson, Edmund. 1970. *Modern Treatment of Tense Patients*. Springfield, IL: Charles C. Thomas.

Machado, Antonio. 1982. *Selected Poems*, trans. Alan S. Trueblood. Cambridge, MA: Harvard University Press.

Sheets-Johnstone, Maxine. 1999/expanded 2nd ed. 2011. *The Primacy of Movement*, vol. 14, Advances in Consciousness Research. Amsterdam/Philadelphia: John Benjamins Publishing.

Stern, Daniel N. 1985. *The Interpersonal World of the Infant: A View from Psychoanalysis and Developmental Psychology*. New York: Basic Books.

Notes

Notes

Notes

Notes

Notes

Notes

31590693R00117

Made in the USA
Middletown, DE
08 May 2016